Stephen Clements was
born in Carrickfergus
in 1972, where he now
lives with his wife and
two children. At the
age of thirty-seven he
walked away from a
successful career in
sales to follow his dream
of being on the radio. He
now presents Northern
Ireland's best breakfast
show on Q Radio with
Cate Conway. *Back In
Our Day* is his first book.

# STEPHEN CLEMENTS

# BACK IN OUR DAY

Caravanning in Portrush, slippery-dipping in Newcastle, and other stuff we did growing up in Northern Ireland

·THE·
BLACK
·STAFF
PRESS

First published in 2017 by
Blackstaff Press
an imprint of Colourpoint Creative Limited
Colourpoint House
21 Jubilee Road
Newtownards
Northern Ireland
BT23 4YH

Printed in Antrim by W. & G. Baird

A CIP catalogue record for this book is available from the British Library

ISBN 978-085640-999-8

www.blackstaffpress.com

To my family,
especially to Natasha,
Poppy and Robbie,
for allowing me
moments to nip out of
the house, out of the
twenty-first century and
to step back in time.

# CONTENTS

# FOREWORD
## BY COLIN MURRAY

I first properly met Stephen Clements when he helped drum up support for my mankini walk through Belfast City Centre on Boxing Day 2015. This came about after I tweeted, 'If Northern Ireland qualify for Euro 2016 I'll run thru Belfast in a green mankini. Without any shame whatsoever.'

From the minute Stephen welcomed me on air to promote the event, his enthusiasm was infectious, his ability to drum up interest and help raise money for a good cause was sensational and, I can comfortably state, his radio skills are a match for anyone's. This is not an empty platitude. I genuinely think he's a brilliant radio presenter.

Not only did he help me to raise awareness of the event and money, but he donned a mankini himself and joined me on the walk, which sums up the man himself. Seeing him turn up almost naked that morning told me two things: 1) his enthusiasm and support were genuine and 2) he's lucky he has a good sense of humour.

There's more evidence of that sense of humour in this book. It's a brisk ramble through childhood and coming of age in Northern Ireland which will make any working-class person from our neck of the woods smile. A lot.

From Barry's to binbags, from White Lightning to woodchip wallpaper, there were countless paragraphs that sent me straight back to the Moat Park in Dundonald, or to the time I got in trouble for picking the wood-chip off my bedroom wall.

The book will make you reminisce about something with a friend, or simply day-dream back about something you'd forgotten about as you grew older. I enjoyed these moments immensely, whether they made me laugh or, on occasion, made me a little sentimental.

My favourite reference was to Mojos! We'd go into Menzie's in Ballybeen and we'd get 20 for 10p! Even then, we were such wee shites that we'd try to get an extra one past the owner, knowing that if he did a random spot-check and discovered it, he'd go mental and buck us out of the shop.

This book is also a stark reminder of just how ridiculously un-PC some things were back in the day, although at the time they seemed normal. Ladies on cans of Tennent's anyone? Thank goodness we've moved on.

I must also be honest and say that some parts of this book disgusted me, none more so than Clements's blatant slagging of Yellow Pack crisps – and eulogising instead the likes of posh gammon & pineapple Tudor Specials which, as anyone reading this knows, were a betrayal of potato-based snacks everywhere. In actual fact, I lived for salt and vinegar Yellow Pack, and I'll be giving the author a good old-fashioned skelpin' the next time I see him.

Suffice to say, this read is like Stephen himself – warm, genuine, funny and straight to the point. And, just as you would with Stephen, you will be all the better off for being in its company.

*Colin Murray*

# INTRODUCTION

We all do it. Reminisce until we almost ache with nostalgia. The first time it happens it's almost as if the words are coming out without your permission. Watching a concert on TV, for example: 'Sure, it's so obvious they're miming parts of that song. When I was young that would nev ...' And you stop dead in your tracks.

It's happened. You've become your mum, dad, auntie, uncle, granda or nana. It doesn't matter who you've become, it just matters that it's happened. You have crossed a threshold and at first you deny it. Like the first grey hair you find – it's not really grey. It's the light bouncing off it. The sun did it. I fell asleep against a freshly painted wall.

But you know. We ALL know.

Policemen start to look like boy scouts with guns. Teachers start to look like students. Politicians? We went to school with their parents (not all of them, of course – we do like to keep a few dinosaurs to help us feel comfortable).

The exciting part is embracing it! It's a rite of passage after all. We've paid our dues (if not our mortgages yet) and it's our God-given right to look back through rose-tinted glasses at our past.

In Northern Ireland our glasses are heavily tinted. There is no doubt that a lot of our past is not particularly rose tinted. We all know the saying here that there is not one person who hasn't been affected by the Troubles in one way or another.

In many ways, the very darkest days of the past have helped shape us all into who we are now. Regardless of where we grew up, which school we went to, which team we supported or which church or chapel we were forced to go to, we all have one thing in common: our ferociously dark sense of humour.

Which made the offer to write about the good old days in Northern Ireland one I simply couldn't refuse!

I'm at that age now where the *Topcat* TV theme tune, the cover of a Ladybird book, the smell of dulse, or even my mum (still) scolding me for not turning the kitchen light off can instantly take me back ... back to the good old days.

# Chapter One
# HOLIDAYS

# PORTRUSH

'Right, boys. Here's your summer outfits and new trainers. We're heading to … Portrush in a caravan for a fortnight!'

Summer holidays were always brilliant. As I recall, through the rose-tinters, the weather was always amazing. Always. Thirty degrees for the full two months that we were off.

So off to Portrush we'd go. First thing, it was 'a drive' – a few hours up the coastal route in the back of my dad's Ford Capri from Carrickfergus to Portrush. It was cramped back there, and roasting, and we were made to listen to the current *Top of the Pops* tape – which featured the most sexist album covers ever seen – and

*Top of the Pops* albums were the best. The music was okay too.

Silky skills at the caravan in Portrush. (Note the massive terry-towelling NI sweatbands.)

a Rolling Stones album that had been taped from the vinyl. I still sing 'Start Me Up' with a hint of warp from where the tape had been sun damaged, and I still know every word to Rod Stewart's 'Maggie May'.

So we arrive at the caravan and the first thing we do is scream, 'BARRY'S', to which Mum and Dad in unison say, 'NO. In the morning. Go and explore.'

Now, exploring was something we did as kids back then. Exploring was a pastime in itself. And we didn't need to be somewhere fancy-pants like Portrush. Anywhere was fair game. My brother and I regularly went exploring in places that would send cold shivers up and down the spines of parents these days. To be fair, our parents never knew enough to get cold shivers. But that's because we didn't have to tell them precise locations. 'Do not go across the big road. Do not speak to strange people. Be back before the lights come on.' They were the rules.

Burnt orange was the height of caravanning fashion. The sound system was a battery-powered transistor radio.

I remember being *told* (in case anyone who works for the PSNI or Graham Construction is reading this) about two young boys who managed to start a dumper truck and drive it into the wall of a half-built house on a construction site near Carrickfergus. Honestly. Can't even bear to think about what might have happened. But we were exploring. Sorry, *they* were exploring.

So back to Cairn Dhu caravan park, circa 1981, which – by the way – is the worst place to take kids. You can see Portrush. You can smell Portrush. But without your parents, you can't get to Portrush. Off we went, exploring. Couple of older kids. Immediately scared of them. Big kids were bad. They were always bad and they always will be bad. They will steal your Pacers, they will burst your football, they will take your Grifter and race it into the wall, they are generally just evil. But that's their job.

We give the older kids a bye-ball and see a couple of girls our age. Eeeeuuuuugh. Go away, Sandra. No, you can't play football with us. We hate girls. (This changed dramatically just a few years later, when we'd have handed over our football for a bit of QT with Sandra.)

That was another thing from back in the day. Everyone had real names. Gordon, Andrew, Simon, Sandra, Louise and so on. There was a Pippa in our school at one stage but I'm fairly sure she changed her name to Elsie due to the ribbing she took.

So, exploring done – caravan parks back then had nothing in them bar caravans – we returned to what would be our home for the next two weeks.

The burnt-orange-and-chocolate décor was an instant hit. 'This place is nicer than our house.' Standard first impression. Beds chosen and summer outfits unpacked (tight shorts, stripy T-shirts, Gola trainers), we all sat down, ready for dinner.

'Let's get a chippy!'

'YES!!'

The only chip shop anywhere nearby was on the main street in

Holiday staple diet of fish and chips. It didn't get much better.

A kind of weird early hobby-horse-type thing. Note the hard stony surface for maximum knee-cutting potential if you fell.

Portrush which meant a chance, just a chance, of ten minutes in Sportsland or Phil's Amusements. Chips bought and demolished, we asked could we just have a wee look in Phil's. We were on holiday and Mum and Dad's strictness dissolved with every salt-and-vinegar-soaked chip they ate. 'Away you go, then, but stay where we can see you.'

Green light! We had been saving for months for this trip and had the guts of £11 each to do us the two weeks. First stop, the change counter. Turned our crumpled £1 note into fifty two-pence pieces. Rappers like 50 Cent think they invented that kinda cool walk with a limp that they do while grabbing their crotches. Nah, mate! We were doing that as we limped

**Start Me Up, The Rolling Stones**
**Maggie May, Rod Stewart**
**Don't Go Breaking My Heart, Elton John and Kiki Dee**
**Lovely Day, Bill Withers**
**Don't Stop Me Now, Queen**
**Go Your Own Way, Fleetwood Mac**
**Under Pressure, Queen and David Bowie**
**The Winner Takes It All, ABBA**
**Take On Me, a-ha**
**Driving in My Car, Madness**

**HOLIDAYS MIX TAPE**

up to the one-armed bandits, holding our shorts up due to the weight of the 2ps.

After we had gambled all our money away with zero luck, it was back to the caravan for everyone. The holiday hadn't even really started yet but we were already loving life. A bellyful of chips, and we'd managed to get in to Phil's. The promise of the beach in the morning and Barry's in the afternoon was almost too exciting. Before bed, though, it was time for a quick game of Snakes and Ladders with ... a sweet treat. Winner!

We were never allowed sweet treats before bed but I suspect that Mum and Dad knew that nothing could keep us awake after running around all night exploring and gambling. Out came a finger of Fudge each. Everyone burst into song – which was actually mandatory in the 80s if anyone got the finger out. Dad was on a Picnic bar. (We **NEVER** wanted a bit of Dad's Picnic – it had raisins in it, for God's sake! And nuts. If we wanted a salad we'd have asked for one.) Mum, on the other hand, brought out the 'posh choc'. Fry's Five Centres.

Wow! This was like the moment in *Charlie and the Chocolate Factory*

when Charlie sees a Wonka Bar for the first time. As these were normally consumed past our bedtime, this was a rare sighting indeed. Five flavours in one bar.

But Gavin and I knew we couldn't ask. Shouldn't ask. In those days, you took what you were given, and you were (genuinely) thankful. But come on! Each piece Mum broke off was a different colour. A judgement call had to be made. I knew what to do.

'Mum, Gavin wants to know if we can have a bit of your chocolate?'

'No, I didn't. I'm telling. It's you that wants some.'

I give Gavin a slap for not mind-reading my cunning plan. He was younger and therefore the more likely of the two of us to get a piece. Dick.

'Mum! Stephen's hitting me.'

Chaos ensues. Dad loses the rag and takes all chocolate off the table. 'Spoilt wee shites, the pair of ya.'

Gavin's whimpering cry escalated quickly to a wail.

I also began to cry at the complete and utter unfairness of it all. 'I don't even want the stupid chocolate anyway.' My inner voice is screaming, 'Mistake, mistake, mistake.' Dad reaches across the table, snakes and ladders everywhere, and grabs me by the collar of my Primark jammies. 'You're one ungrateful wee shite. Right, Helen, come on. Pack up. We're going home. And shut up and stop crying or do you want me to give you something to cry about?'

To this day I'm still not sure what this means. I never really was sure if I was supposed to answer or not. This is the kind of trick question you won't encounter again in your life until you get a bit older and head on to the dating scene and hear the words, 'Do these trousers make my bum look big?'

Anyway, by this stage both Gavin and I sound like car alarms. Mum and Dad are bluffing, of course, but we don't know that. We think the dream is over. 'Get to your beds while we pack the Capri.' We fall asleep. That deep sleep you only ever experience as a child. That deeper sleep you only ever experience as a child who's been crying right up to the moment they fall asleep.

The dream wasn't over, though. It hadn't even begun!

P.S. To this day I've never tried a Fry's Five Centres. And I'm not sure I ever will. Anyone I asked said they're minging anyway.

The Ford Cortina RAMMED with food, clothes and family.

'Barry's, Barry's, Barry's!' The chant. It was actually happening. We were in the Capri, TOTP blaring, looking for a parking space.

You see Barry's WAS Disneyland to us back in the day. Disney didn't even bother advertising on TV here because nobody could afford it. Actually, there may have been one advert that went out once, but it was met with 'Ahhhh, for God's sake! Sure, that would cost more than our house' by parents across the land. Disneyland was some sort of distant dream. This was the reality! (The Disney slot was handed to Spar, I believe, who got a free 'Fred, there's no bread' ad in its place.)

'Okay. You've got £2 each to last you all day. Don't come asking for more.'

It was all about strategy. Get some of the money changed into 2ps and look around for the one-armed bandits or – even better – those wee slider machines. On many occasions we accidentally 'bumped' into them, hoping for a quick win. The machines weighed the guts of 3 ½ tonnes ... It was rare that that approach would work, although on the odd occasion you'd be casually walking past and a few 2ps would drop from nowhere. Win.

So off we went. The big rides were out. Mum and Dad paid for those and

Some early gambling when you had to physically pull the one-armed bandit's one arm. As time passed, the pulling of the arm was considered an inconvenience and they were replaced by buttons. (Note sweatbands, again, to wipe away the fear when down to my last few 2ps.)

The putting green at Ramore Head in Portrush. Sky blue trousers were the height of fashion.

we could choose one to go on before we left. They didn't come from the £2.

It was all about the melons. Looking back, not a whole lot changed between the Portrush holiday and the Kavos lads' vacation later on. The eternal – and often futile – search for melons, but at Barry's we were looking for three in a row. Gavin and I would be putting the 2ps in like nobody's business. It was us against the blue-rinse grannies. They watched what we were doing – really watched – like they knew something we didn't.

I hated those wee smoky grannies. Pumping 2ps into two machines at once, dipping into a never-ending supply of coins from their wee handbags, only stopping when a lemon bonbon was dislodged and fell to the floor. The five-second rule applied even back then and, quite often, teeth would be removed and bonbon popped into the mouth with the speed and dexterity of some sort of sweet-eating ninja.

We never really won much, or lost much, but the noise and smell of Barry's was intoxicating. We ran about like we were in heaven. We were in heaven! Portrush rock, candyfloss made in front of your eyes (never pre-made in a bucket) by some sort of Harry Potter-esque wizard with nothing bar pink sugar, a stick and an upturned barrel.

Looking back, the rides were mainly pretty crap. The ghost train wasn't that scary – I've had scarier phone bills – but we had nothing to compare it to, so a couple of rubber masks and a rubbish skeleton could have made anyone cry and maybe pee their Y-fronts a little. Not me. I never peed a little into my Captain Pugwash pants. Anyone who tells you different is lying* (*may not be lying).

I learnt to swim in Portrush. Thinking back, this is an unreasonable way to teach anyone to swim. The sea there is the Atlantic after all. I think Greenland is next, if you head north.

'Go on in, ya big Jinny-Anns!' Gavin and I didn't even know what a Jinny-Ann was, but we sure didn't want to be one. I don't think I have ever felt pain like it since. The searing ice-cold pressure on our foreheads was one of the reasons we learnt to swim so quickly. Under no circumstances did we want to put our heads under the water again.

Speedos. That is all.

# NEWCASTLE

**It wasn't just Portrush. There was Newcastle as well. Always freezing. Always.**

Newcastle never had the same allure as Portrush as there was no Disneyland (aka Barry's) but it was still a place of wonder. The Slippery Dip is surely one of the best, and most famous, slides of all time. Get into an itchy scratchy hessian sack and then race your friends down the track at speeds of up to 55 mph. Another hessian mat at the bottom stopped you so violently that if you didn't leave the slide with some sort of semi-permanent burn, you weren't going fast enough. Some snotty teen at the bottom would say, 'You okay?' (he didn't care), and through streaming eyes as you wiped the thick fibres from your bloodied knees you'd shout, 'YEEESSS! MORE!'

Two letters spell Ireland's favourite ice cream.

**TOP 10 ICE LOLLIES**
1. Fab
2. Dracula
3. That-A-Way
4. Rocky Rasper
5. Fat Frog
6. Screwball
7. JR
8. Zoom
9. Feast
10. Loop the Loop

The most fun to be had in a hessian sack. You'd be picking fibres out of your knees for weeks afterwards.

# AT HOME

Summer holidays as a kid were about calling for your mates. No phones – we didn't even have a house phone when I was young – and the closest we came to mobile phones were yoghurt pots with string between them or a calculator flipped open while we pretended to be Captain Kirk and Spock.

We had to call for our friends. Like walk/run/cycle to their house and ask if they were in. Sometimes it was miles and when you got there, out of breath, panting, 'Is … Peter … in …?' you'd be met with, 'No, Stephen, he's away to your house to call for you.'

Fuck (is what we thought back then but never said). 'Okay, Mrs Gardner, thank you very much, please, thank you.' We were taught manners and woe betide us if we were caught being rude or disrespectful. And that didn't just mean that you'd get a clip from your own mum or dad. Your mates' parents were allowed to give you a clip too. Right or wrong, that's the way it was.

Once we'd finally tracked each other down, our group of mates spent hours on our bikes. We built jumps from pieces of wood and breeze blocks we found – really just ramps – and someone had to lie under the jump while someone else rode over it. To be part of the gang, you had to take your turn beneath the jump. We took turns. To be a part of the gang you HAD to take your turn. There are few things in life scarier than sitting up at a 30 degree angle to check how close Alan Gilmore is to ramp impact, to see him coming at you at 30 mph on a Chopper. I still think I have a Grifter tyre-print on my outer thigh from this.

Roller skates were mainly for girls but we tried them. They looked like bear traps – they were a kind of metal contraption you stuck your gutties into and then tightened the red leather strap around. And when you pulled that strap, you pulled tight. Trying to skate like Torvill and Dean was difficult enough, but nothing was worse than gaining a bit of momentum only to find that the red leather strap had come loose and, just as you reached some decent speed, being stopped in your tracks by your next foot plant. More blood, more tears, more plasters.

Nothing could stop us, though. Nothing slowed us down; nothing could make us come indoors. The TV was rubbish – even *Why Don't You?* was always crap, apart from the opening sequence when we all tried to sing the fast bit. We only came in for food (usually jam sandwiches), drink (usually cordial) and the toilet (usually ... although trees were an option).

Sometimes, we would simply dig holes. I can't remember if there was actually a reason for it here – there probably wasn't!

Mum helping out getting the BMXs ready for the day. Notice the GT California with black mags I am riding. It took a gold chain and £30 I'd saved from my paper round to get this from Steenson.

# IPSOS

Then we got older. Summer holidays, in particular, changed. We spent them mainly trying to avoid being caught drinking. I'm fairly sure most people in Northern Ireland did cracking Ian Paisley impressions back in the day, trying to talk to their parents through a mouthful of Polo mints. Very whistle-y.

Cider was usually the drink of choice and it was nothing like these fancy apple drinks poured perfectly over ice that everyone has now. I'm talking about two, sometimes three, litres of lukewarm White Lightning (or Strongbow if you were quite posh) and we drank them as quickly as physically possible. Quite often we shared them around, slabbers everywhere – absolutely disgusting. Like a teenage version of the Hallowe'en apple bobbing, in many ways.

When we did eventually start getting out of the country for a 'forn holiday' it was a very different experience to what it is now.

I went on my first-ever proper forn holiday with my mate Lawrence to Ipsos in Corfu. It may seem like a strange destination, and in many ways it was, but it came about like this.

We used to work in the summers at Henderson's in Mallusk, loading lorries and the like. Every Friday we received our pay cheques and headed straight to the Northern Bank to wait in the queue to get her cashed.

One Friday we decided that we'd take our wad of cash and head to the travel agents in Northcott, Newtownabbey. **WHAP**. We landed £450 on the desk of the girl in the shop.

Lawrence and I enjoying the beach with all the friends we made.

'Can we go somewhere with that, where there are loads of girls and no families and it's sunny?'

'Let's have a look. Ipsos?'

'Sounds good – we'll take it.'

And that's how we booked holidays. No internet in those days. You made sure you had your tickets, your passports and your cash. (Not too much – you always had the majority in travellers cheques as forners would likely steal your cash, but were less likely to steal your cheques, apparently.)

So off we went and it was fantastic. Forn holidays were not something many people did and we felt like millionaires! Arriving at the airport to be hit by that wall of heat, something we all are used to now, was an incredible feeling back then. I remember getting on the bus with lots of other holidaymakers and waiting ages to get to our apartments.

The after effects of cheap wine and moussaka.

It was late in the evening and the bus stopped at loads of cracker places – super-cool apartments – to let people out. As we climbed a very steep hill out of the centre of Ipsos, Lawrence and I both laughed quietly.

'Wonder which dickheads have been stitched up here? Middle of fucking nowhere ...'

'For fuck's sake, shhhhh. They could be sitting behi—'

'Mr and Mrs Clements, this is your stop,' screamed the hyper holiday rep over the tannoy.

Christ. This place was ours. And the Mr and Mrs Clements bit had certainly done us no favours with any of the girls that we'd spotted on the coach. Anyway, we were here, and it was warm, and it was time to party.

There were no mobile phones back then so you always had to ring home from a landline (if you could find one) and let your parents know you'd arrived safely. A let-it-ring-twice-and-hang-up would not suffice for this international trip.

Once we'd called home, it was straight to the nearest beach bar. This was paradise. We vaguely remembered some gorgeous English bar rep girl saying, 'Don't go too mad on your first night – the heat and the drink can really hit you.'

QUALITY CONTROL
Red/Yellow overall cast to prints
Film exposed under tungsten light, or early
morning/late afternoon sunlight
Warning: Fluorescent lights give prints a
yellow/green cast
ADVICE LABEL

LIFT & PEEL HERE

QUALITY CONTROL
Blurred out of focus prints
• Camera shake - hold camera steady
• Focussing error - applies to variable focus cameras
• Subject too close - allow 2 metre distance for fixed
focus cameras
• Dirt or condensation on lens
ADVICE LABEL

Yeah, what does she know? We're from Belfast; we DRINK; that's what we do.

So the next morning, as we sat showing her the stitches in my knee from where I'd fallen off the side of the road laughing at Lawrence, who was showing her the bruise on the side of his head from when a slow-moving bus had hit him, we had some humble pie for breakfast. Well, humble pie and a beer. We were on holiday, after all.

The next couple of weeks were a blur after that. Our only memories were sparked by photographs that we couldn't wait to get the hold of. Actual physical photos. There was no digital and no filters. You also had absolutely no clue what they would look like until you collected them from Boots.

We came home, took the films to Boots and waited the week, or fortnight, or whatever it was to see the carnage. We could have paid £10 or something to get them done in an hour but nobody had that kind of spare cash.

The waiting and the looking through was one of the highlights from any holiday. Meeting up and arranging to go to town to collect them. The look of absolute disgust on the face of the (always) old woman who had seen all our snaps and had put little *Poor Quality* stickers on the crap ones. And worse, who had put little tiny *In Poor Taste* stickers over the offensive ones. #facepalm didn't exist back then but we would have done it if it did. I always felt like justifying the 'offensive' stickers: 'That girl's boobs were just in the background. We didn't realise they were in shot.'

They weren't and we did.

'It looks like I'm snogging that older woman but I'm not.'

I was.

'In my defence, it was very cold when that photo was taken.'

It wasn't.

Sometimes I feel for this current generation. They will never have a bad photo due to digital snaps, instant editing, deleting and filtering. But they will also never experience the tears of laughter, the mortification, the pure joy of looking through your holiday snaps and remembering things, events and people that oftentimes you'd no recollection of.

# Chapter Two

# GOING INTO TOWN

# BELFAST CITY CENTRE

**Shopping was a completely different experience back then compared to now. We nearly always went out to get something. There was little or no spare money so if we were going to go to Belfast, for example, there was always a reason.**

This was back when all towns closed at 6 p.m. And by closed, I mean closed. Locked. Barriers down. Military on the streets with guns.

SHUT.

Even if you arrived in the daytime, there were barriers to get through. To get into Belfast city centre, in particular, you were searched and then you had to get through something like a turnstile at a football stadium. All of this under the watchful gaze of the British Army and the RUC, every one heavily armed with handguns, and automatic and semi-automatic machine guns. Getting into town was difficult. At peak times, there could be queues for goodness' sake! Queueing to get into a city just to shop. It was kind of like a cross between an airport and the cinema. With firearms.

A kid nowadays would think the shops were crap, but to us they were amazing. They were almost all independently owned, mainly because a lot of the big chains deemed NI too risky and so it was left to the local businesses to supply us with our goods. Okay, there were the odd exceptions, and as time passed, more and more arrived, but for a great deal of the 70s and into the 80s, it was locally owned businesses serving the local shoppers.

One exception was Boots, which is still in the same place on Donegall Place. I remember being very young

**Fashion, David Bowie**
**Two Tribes, Frankie Goes to Hollywood**
**Hot in the City, Billy Idol**
**Bad, Michael Jackson**
**The Power of Love, Huey Lewis and the News**
**Pink Panther theme**
**There's a Guy Works Down the Chip Shop Swears He's Elvis, Kirsty MacColl**
**Upside Down, Diana Ross**
**When the Going Gets Tough, Billy Ocean**
**We Built This City, Starship**

**GOING INTO TOWN MIX TAPE**

·Please Fold·
Umbrellas
Before Entering
Check

**Bus Search Point Only**

The entrance to Belfast city centre was akin to the way airport security is these days. Only with heavily armed military personnel. There were still conductors on some of the buses back then, too.

and heading through the barriers with my mum and my late Aunt Irene. Irene was one of the most beautiful, funny, kind and positive people I have ever had the privilege of knowing and loving.

I never really liked Boots as a kid, or as an adult for that matter, as there was nothing there for me bar an aisle that LOOKED like it was full of toys, but on closer inspection (and with a huge amount of disappointment) turned out to be stacked with different types of soaps with characters printed on them. Mickey on a rope. Yoda on a rope. Pink Panther on a rope. Scooby on a rope. Dress it up how you want, it was soap – and a standard Christmas present from distant relatives. Not something you could play with, so instantly dismissed.

Anyway, on this occasion, whilst approaching the door to Boots, Mum and Irene were busy chatting away and not really paying attention to their surroundings. On autopilot so to speak. Even though we'd already been through the security check at the gates, we'd also have been searched at the door of most of the shops. How long and how fierce this search was correlated exactly with how dodgy you looked.

Mum and Irene always looked close to but not quite Sunday best when out shopping and therefore would have

Seems incredible now, but you used to have your bag searched on the WAY IN to towns and cities, never mind going into the shops.

Athletic Stores in Belfast. The only place in Northern Ireland at the time that I knew of that did away kits for Man Utd. We used to go in just to look at them.

been deemed low risk. They knew this and approached the door casually, not looking up, just getting ready for the quick search that was about to happen.

I could see that the security guard was busy checking the handbags and so I watched, confused, as my Aunt Irene walked up to a man and flung open her knee-length coat. Irene was a strikingly beautiful woman, and she was wearing a dress underneath that, without her knowing, would have stopped grown men in their tracks. She was as beautiful on the outside as she was on the inside.

The man looked her up and down and went bright red before embarrassedly mumbling, 'Thanks very much, luv, but I don't work here.'

Irene and my mum cried with laughter the rest of the day at her aggressive-flasher approach to the poor wee man who was having a sneaky feg outside Boots whilst, no doubt, waiting for the Mrs to come out with a bottle of Anais Anais or something.

Boots was most definitely a 'mum' store. There was very little in there to interest a young boy, but the payoff was that we always went to Athletic Stores to see the football tops. That's what we did anyway. They had almost every team you could name plus the odd time you could see a Barcelona or Real Madrid top. Nowhere else sold these!

It was also the only place that I knew of, that had the **LONG SLEEVE TOP** just like the players would wear sometimes and also the only place **ON PLANET EARTH** that ever sold the 'third' kit of any team. I still remember actually stroking the blue Manchester United top that I'd only ever seen the likes of Bryan Robson wearing on TV, with all the reverence of a violinist handling a Stradivarius.

# WOOLWORTHS

**If you wanted the latest music, you had a few options. My favourite was Woolworths as there was always a chance you'd get a rattle at the Pic 'n' Mix, although this was a risky affair from a parent's point of view – you were only told the price once your bag was weighed.**

By then you were already in the queue and no mum or dad would **EVER** be seen to back down from paying.

Parents realised that the kids were on to something and so many times you'd hear mums whispering through gritted smiles, 'Don't you feckin' **DARE** lift too much.' We learned to go for quantity on things like UFOs (rice paper circles in the shape of flying saucers filled with sherbet) and appreciated the quality – so only went for a few – of stuff like giant strawberries.

Woolies was **THE** place for music as it usually had the Top 40 singles. Way back when, these were all 7-inch vinyls, soon to be joined by cassingles (cassette singles with a cardboard sleeve) and later by CD singles (costing £4.99 each?!?!?!). There was Golden Discs, HMV, and later the Virgin MegaStore, which was an absolute mammoth of a music retail outlet. I remember when it opened you were able to listen to some tracks on headphones. It was like walking on to the set of *Back to the Future*, for goodness' sake.

Very few famous singers ever dared come to Northern Ireland, so these giant posters were as close as many of us ever got to seeing them.

# INSHOPS

The first shopping mall that I remember opening in town was InShops. This was just like the shopping malls you would get in America.

Said no one ever. It was pretty shit. At the start, though, it was amazing to us. Loads of actual shops all under one roof. Clothes, shoes, hairdressers, tattoo artists, a pet shop, music and food. The roof was low, the smell of smoke was overpowering but we LOVED it. Especially the food bit.

At the centre of this world of wonder, where all the pathways merged, was the 'food court': Chinese, traditional chippy, American burger joint, Indian, American chicken joint and a kebab joint all in one place. Amazing.

In the second half of InShops' lifespan, long after CastleCourt had come into town and blown it away, the number of eateries dwindled to maybe three or four max, and regardless of which place you went to, you were served by the same man.

You'd be looking up at the Chinese menu wondering, look down and there would be a fella standing. 'What's yours, son?'

'Mmmm ... not sure.'

Move along a few steps to the right to look at the American diner menu ...

'What's yours, son?'

WHAT!

'It's you again.'

'And wha?'

Once you'd got over the shock and ordered he would go back into the kitchen where he would become the 'chef', clatter around, and then return to his original job – 'waiter' – and bring you out whatever you'd decided on. Unsurprisingly, everything tasted like age-old NI chippy food with either a fried chicken wing, kebab meat or rice thrown on top.

# CURFEWS, PEDESTRIANISED AREAS AND SMOKE-DAMAGE SALES

Another thing about town in those days was that it was a largely pedestrian experience. Not because we all wanted to dander about willy-nilly in an environment free from pollution, but because cars weren't allowed into town.

Delivery and military vehicles, and buses were all that were allowed in, unless for a very good reason. In the provincial towns it was slightly different – there was a curfew and all cars had to be out by that time. If you didn't get your Ford Cortina away, there was a good chance that the next time you'd see it would be on the news as the boot was blown up by a wee robot thing on wheels. The controlled explosion claimed many a shit car during these times.

There is no avoiding the fact that there were many bombs on commercial premises. Nine times out of ten the whole country would know where and when the next 'fire and smoke damage

January sales, spring sales, summer sales and bomb damage sales ... they all seemed normal to us.

sale' would be. If, in the middle of a show like *Corrie*, a banner scrolled across the bottom of the screen that read, 'Could key holders in Main Street Portadown please contact Portadown RUC station,' well, then you knew.

I do remember a family member, who shall remain nameless, saying, 'Ooh, there's a lovely wee furniture shop there, and they'd a lovely pouffe I had my eye on ...' Rumours persisted for years that some of the smaller incendiaries were 'to order' so to speak. Maybe someone had spotted some lovely porcelain dogs that would've looked sweet on the hearth but couldn't afford them unless ...

**TOP 10 CARS**
1  Audi Quattro
2  Ford Capri
3  Ford Escort XR3i Mk 3
4  DeLorean
5  Vauxhall Nova (The spided-up-to-the-max edition.)
6  Ford Orion (Shit, but my dad got one with work and we loved it!)
7  Ford Sierra
8  Mini Metro
9  Vauxhall Chevette
10  Ford Cortina

Chapter Three
# BIG DAYS

# HALLOWE'EN

Let's start with Americans. Yes. It's their fault that basic holidays have changed into what they are now.

Back in the day, Hallowe'en was a very simple and short-lived affair. These days Hallowe'en is scarier than the Hammer House of Horrors, for God's sake! The costumes available today are unbelievable, never mind the make-up! On several occasions I've almost called 999, thinking I was a witness to some sort of terrible accident, only to see the 'victims' – with faces hanging off and limbs swinging in the wind – necking bottles of Buckfast and eating monkey nuts. At least I hope that group were dressed for Hallowe'en, otherwise I would have seemed fairly heartless as I walked by and said, 'Looking good, guys'.

At Hallowe'en, the first thing to sort was an outfit! There were a few options as far as masks went – Dracula, Frankenstein, skeleton and werewolf (which always looked a little too much like a teddy bear so was instantly dismissed). There were, of course, girl masks but it wasn't worth the absolutely devastating death you'd get from your mates to even bother looking. All of these masks had one thing in common. They were in no way frightening! At all. Actually, they had two things in common – they weren't scary, and they were designed to cut and nip you in and around the upper ear area. Whatever way the elastic band attached to the hole on the side of the mask, it always made a slight nick in the plastic, which always cut your ear. You can still tell people's age if you have a wee check just around their ears – if they've a small scar, they grew up here in the 70s and 80s.

Breathing was difficult, the condensation left you all but blind

Not sure if the girl mask was
meant to be scary or not,
but it ended up being more
frightening than the gormless
skeleton. Note the carved
turnip – pumpkins were only
very rarely sighted before the
turn of the century.

with sweat (I don't think I've ever suffered from face sweat since), and the elastic band trapped tight against your head was the earliest form of hair removal known to modern man. Anyway, once the mask had been purchased, it was on to the costume.

There were no costumes. There were bin bags and sheets. You could just about get away with a bin bag for Count Dracula's cape, but even the most creative visionary would have found it difficult to envisage a man turning into a wolf, and halfway through the process – 'Grooooowl … grrrrrrr … awhoooo … oh, a black plastic sheet! Perfect. I'll wear this.'

We didn't care. We were dressed and ready for phase one of Hallowe'en: Hallowe'en rhyming. These days, kids come to the door like extras from Michael Jackson's 'Thriller' – limbs hanging off, blood everywhere, and then they ruin everything with 'trick or treat'. Who'd ever opt for a trick? So they just walk away with a treat. I have to say, I feel cheated in many ways.

In OUR day, you had to know the rhyme.

*Hallowe'en is coming and the geese are getting fat,*
*Please put a penny in the old man's hat.*
*If you haven't got a penny, a ha'penny will do,*
*If you haven't got a ha'penny then God bless you.*

We had to learn that. And there were no sweets involved. We were in it for the cash. Now, it was never very much cash, and looking back,

Dracula and witch were standard go-to outfits. The scariest part of this photo is the creepy doll on top of the 'good glassware and booze' corner unit.

we didn't really set our goals too high. I mean, even back then, a penny wouldn't have got you much, never mind a half-pence piece, but we were in the volume business. We went to every house in the estate. This was not indiscriminate calling either. There was always a plan: hit the big houses first (they were all the same size, but the 'big houses' were those which had a car outside and therefore money).

We hunted in packs. And we always had an ace in every pack. The little brother or sister who for the other 364 days of the year was nothing but a nuisance, was suddenly our biggest asset. The cuteness factor.

'But my not like mask, my not know Hallowe'en coming,' my brother would whimper.

'Shuuuuut upppppp and stand at the front.'

Knock knock.

'Hallowe'en is coming and the geese ...'

'Awk, come here and look, Nigel. Look at the wee dote ...'

RESULT.

Keep pushing my wee brother to the front. Keep pulling his mask down to cover his tear-streaked face. Keep the cash flowing.

'My not want Hallowe'en rhyme. My ears bleeding.'

Shit. He's actually bleeding. What to do? My poor wee brother's ears are actually bleeding and it's about three hours past his bedtime. He's now literally staggering from door to door mumbling incoherently. So I did what all good siblings do.

'If you don't come with us we will leave you out here and that werewolf over there is actually REAL and will eat you alive.'

'But he is wearing a bin bag.'

'Are you suddenly a friggin' expert on werewolves? And stop crying. Werewolves are attracted to *crying*.'

A nod to wee Sid in the werewolf mask who makes an appropriate howling noise – and we are back in the game.

Looking back, it was cruel, but the takings from that one night might have been 20, even 30, per cent of our annual income. At the end of the night, it was back to the house to divvy out the dough. As the oldest, I knew which coins were which, and so it was, 'One for you ($\frac{1}{2}$p) and one for me (50p).' I kept the stupid bit of paper that number 43 had given us. 'You'd think they'd have given us something since he works in a bank.' (It was a £1 note, but the rest didn't know ...)

Hallowe'en was a one-night affair but, before the night arrived, you were always waiting on someone to invite you to a Hallowe'en party – the perfect night was a party and then out for some rhyming. By today's standards these parties were absolutely shit. But we didn't have today's standards then. In fact, when it came to parties, we had no real standards, so they were absolutely brilliant. Except for Christmas and the

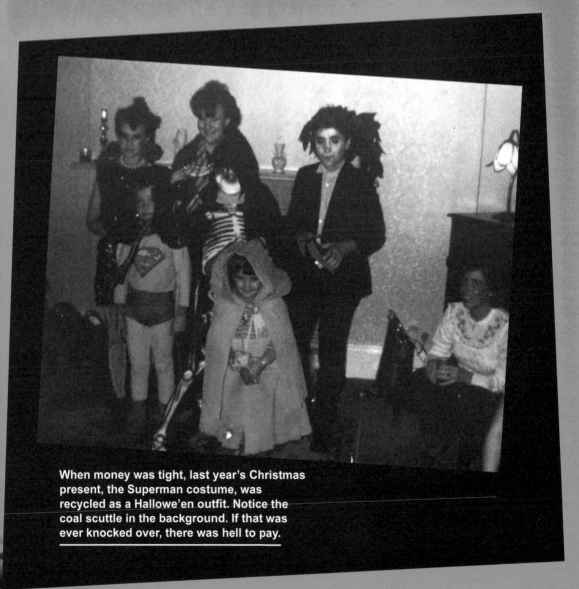

When money was tight, last year's Christmas present, the Superman costume, was recycled as a Hallowe'en outfit. Notice the coal scuttle in the background. If that was ever knocked over, there was hell to pay.

odd birthday party, this was the only en masse celebration in the year and we made the most of it.

The mums and dads were never dressed up as anything but most were semi-cut on Concorde, Babycham or those tins of Tennent's with the half-naked women on the back of them. There was no such thing as political correctness back then. There was also no health and safety. So our games were all either pretty dangerous, or disgusting. But we loved them.

Dunking for apples. Basically, a bucket filled with water with apples floating in it that we had to try and remove with our teeth. So, one by one, with hands behind our backs, we slammed our faces into the bucket to try to 'win' an apple. Bear in mind we all hated apples and, at any other time of year, would have turned up our noses at being given one. But put them in a bucket of what started out as water but after five minutes was probably equal parts water, slabber and snot, we would almost drown just for a bite of the forbidden fruit.

I witnessed kids almost pass out with unconcerned parents shouting, 'Ack, get up da hella that, ya big Jinny-Ann,' while the child writhed breathless on the kitchen floor, regaining consciousness with deep breaths, and with a smile replacing the expression of agony. They had an apple. Towards the end of the night the percentage of water had diminished to almost zero. Pure lukewarm slabber and snot. It didn't stop us. None of our friends ever had eczema or anything, though. Nothing wrong with our immune systems, especially after Hallowe'en.

Then came ... the fireworks! Now, back in the day, it wasn't uncommon to see the sky lit up at night, but that was not due to fireworks as they were banned. Mainly because they could've been used for 'non-fun' purposes. There were always the official fireworks displays around the country but they always felt a little too, well, official. Much better to go to your mate's house, where there were a few Catherine wheels and three rockets that his Aunt Ella had smuggled back from Blackpool on the Liverpool ferry. This was about as exciting as it got! We were breaking the law with adults and we were going to see fireworks.

One year we managed to get our hands on some serious fireworks. I'm fairly sure they came off the back

Ghostbusters, Ray Parker Jr
Thriller, Michael Jackson
The Time Warp, Damian
Rocket Man, Elton John
Driving Home for Christmas, Chris Rea
Merry Christmas Everyone, Shakin' Stevens
Merry Xmas Everybody, Slade
Dukes of Hazzard theme
Last Christmas, Wham!
Fairytale of New York, The Pogues feat. Kirsty MacColl

**BIG DAYS MIX TAPE**

of an unmarked 40-footer that was parked just outside Newry. This year the 'display' was at our house and we could not wait. First things first, get the milk bottle rinsed out. The milk bottle was the holding device for the rockets. It sat proudly at the end of the garden, viewed with the same awe, respect and anticipation as Kennedy Space Centre prior to one of the launches.

'Stand back! He's coming now.'

Dad is making the short, yet ultimately life-threatening, walk of eight feet to the bottom of the garden. In his hands are the rockets and Catherine wheel. They are placed gingerly down to one side, and the first rocket is delicately put in place. Dad kneels down beside it – feg in mouth, which struck me as pretty dangerous even then – takes out his

matches and lights the first match. Here we go …

The wind blows the match out and we all sigh. We can all quite clearly make out 'Ah, for fuck's sake' from Dad, but we pretend we don't. Second attempt – there are some sparks and Dad scrambles to his feet and staggers towards us. 'Get back!'

There's a loud whoosh sound, a whistle that would burst your eardrums and then BANG! There it was – lighting up the street, our faces and scaring the shit out of every pet in a five hundred yard radius. Compared to these days, the firework itself was probably pretty tame. And by tame I mean shit. But to us, who had only the indoor boxed fireworks as a comparison, that was, and remains to this day, the most exciting light show I've ever seen.

# CHRISTMAS

Christmas is also unrecognisable today compared to the old days. We had skinny Santas with cotton wool beards smoking and asking, 'Well, son, what are ya aftur?' in broad NI accents. None of this *Miracle on 34th Street* stuff we have nowadays!

Fantastic lights, houses that are lit up so much you are half-afraid that a Boeing 737 may land in the garden thinking its bloody Aldergrove. Christmas in NI now is what Christmas looked like on TV in our day – not what we experienced.

But Christmas was still everything. There wasn't much in the way of credit back then (bar the Kays catalogue man) so you got what Santa could afford. And Santa's presents always directly reflected the amount of money that was available in your house, which often for my friends and me wasn't much. Here's the thing, though: it never mattered. Until you

got older and started believing the marketing hype – that you needed a pair of 501 jeans – any present was a good present because it was the only time of year you got more than one item gifted to you (the obvious exception being birthdays).

Christmas RULED back in the day.

The run-up started when the *Radio Times* and *TV Times* came out, roughly ten days before the big day. There was to be no mention of it prior to then in the house. Mum and Dad would crack up and Santa WOULD NOT VISIT. As soon as the *Radio Times* was out, we got a copy. This was an event in itself since

Our AMAZING Aunt Eileen modelling the very latest in audio technology, the Walkman. Also seen holding a bottle of cheap fizzy wine for some unknown reason.

Everyone had their own 'Christmas corner' where on the night of the 25th, we would take stock of what Santa had brought us.

My brother and I LITERALLY dressed in our Sunday best, hair freshly washed to go and meet Santa. By the looks of him, he was unimpressed. Note the planetary backdrop, which of course, back in the 80s, had the same festive significance as today. None.

Hats HAD to be worn, be they paper crowns or a disastrous green flat cap from Aunt Eileen. Home-made pavlova and Shloer were the luxuries.

Board games and a new leather football. Despite my sleep-deprived facial expression, I couldn't have been more ecstatic. You can just make out a mini Cadbury dispenser which only lasted until it was finished as nowhere in NI sold replacements.

Gavin and I about to start looking through our toys. We're both wearing our Christmas clothes that we got from Santa – Gavin in a Dallas Cowboys jumper and me in my fake Adidas tracksuit. We LOVED these outfits.

we never got one any other time of year. Gavin and I had it on the floor straight away with our Staedtler Sticks at the ready to circle what we'd be watching.

The movies were never new, but we all watched them and we watched them at the same time as there was no such thing as on demand. So, after Christmas – and all through the year – we all went into school talking about the same things we'd watched, people we liked or didn't like, stuff we'd try on our BMXs at the weekend ... you

know. It was like social media is today in many ways.

But with real people.

And without the photos of dinners.

Or selfies.

Or squirrels surfing.

Actually, it was nothing like social media is today. It involved real people, laughing and arguing and fighting and making up and laughing again, in a real-life three-dimensional world. Young people these days should try it!

As well as TV, Christmas was all about families and Aunt Eileen and Granda falling asleep in the living room, and shit decorations and sending cards and going to ... LEISUREWORLD. If you lived within a 50 mile radius of Belfast, then this Queen Street wonderland was the mecca for toys. I remember the huge teddys that sat downstairs that only movie stars' kids and those whose parents lived in Cultra could afford. Even if we could've managed to get one, it would have taken up about 35 per cent of the downstairs floor space of our house. Nah. Not for us.

But Leisureworld did have Scalextric tracks and Hornby train sets. My brother and I always desperately wanted a Scalextric track! Every year we'd write our list to Santa and most years we got awesome presents, but no Scalextric. I remember one year we got a *Dukes of Hazzard* dress-up set, and we couldn't have been happier dressing up as Boss

Nana, my cousin Simon and me. This is probably Boxing Day. The crockery isn't the good stuff and there are more condiments to mask the taste of leftovers.

Nana, my uncle and Wendy going for 'all you can eat'. Branston Pickle (standard) and home-made Christmas cake on the table alongside matching crockery (another once per year event).

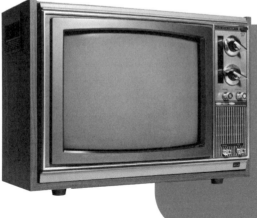

**TOP 10 TV SHOWS**
1 Wonder Woman
2 Swap Shop
3 Worzel Gummidge
4 Record Breakers
5 The Wonder Years
6 The A-Team
7 Knight Rider
8 Monkey
9 The Dukes of Hazzard
10 Starsky & Hutch

Hogg and his daft sheriff, Rosco P. Coltrane. Looking back, these were probably the worst two characters to have been from that show, but it was Christmas and we loved everything we got. At one stage, we even dressed our dog Zico (named after the Brazilian footballer from that great 1982 team) in the Boss Hogg hat.

Back in the day, the presents were simpler and the reactions better. We didn't get as much as kids do these days, so every thing that we did get was special.

When Gavin and I did eventually get a Scalextric – we'd asked for the 'super-fast Formula 1 mental track' – it was the 'round-in-a-circle Ford Escort track' but, let me tell you, that with every ounce of our beings, we loved that present. There weren't as many pictures taken back then, but if there had been a photo of our faces as we ripped off the wrapping paper, you would have seen joy in its purest form. Santa quite regularly would have left us a version of an Adidas tracksuit, but maybe with four stripes and Adidas spelled incorrectly, but we **DID NOT CARE**.

One of my all-time best presents ever was a racer bike. It was purple, had a big mudguard at the back and it arrived right in the middle of the BMX craze so I was not one of the cool kids but, man, I loved that bike! It had ten gears, as I recall, and I used to get up to some serious speeds.

I do remember hitting around 30 mph down the seafront at Carrick. There used to be subways back then with two entrances that ran parallel with the road that you were going to walk (or cycle) under! On one side, there were steps, and on the other, there was a slope (an early attempt at disabled access maybe). They came together at the bottom, which was the entrance to the tunnel, and then there were the same two options on the other side.

So you knew, as you approached, that if the far side had steps, you were on the slope side. But there was one that had a half-step, half-slope arrangement (steps halfway down, then a slope.) I remember the absolute fear as I approached the subway in a blur of purple bike, pale blue shellsuit and smoke billowing from the little tiny brakes, knowing that I had chosen the wrong entry and was about to head down those steps. I pulled the brakes as hard as I could, which didn't have much effect in terms of slowing down, but did mean that my shiny shellsuit slipped me forward off the seat and on to the cross bar of the bike. This was one narrow piece of metal tubing, and never meant to be used as a seat. I bounced the whole way down those steps on that bar and am convinced to this day that this incident is the main reason my voice has remained like a high-pitched chipmunk's.

I was Boss Hogg, equipped with pretend walkie-talkie, and Gavin was California Highway Patrol (CHiPs!!). Notice all the Christmas cards that had been received were fixed to the wall, at an angle, with either Blu Tack or Sellotape.

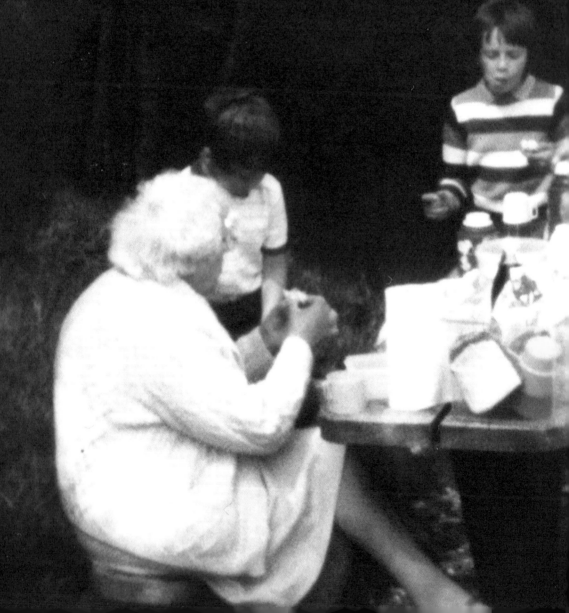

# Chapter Four
# EATING...

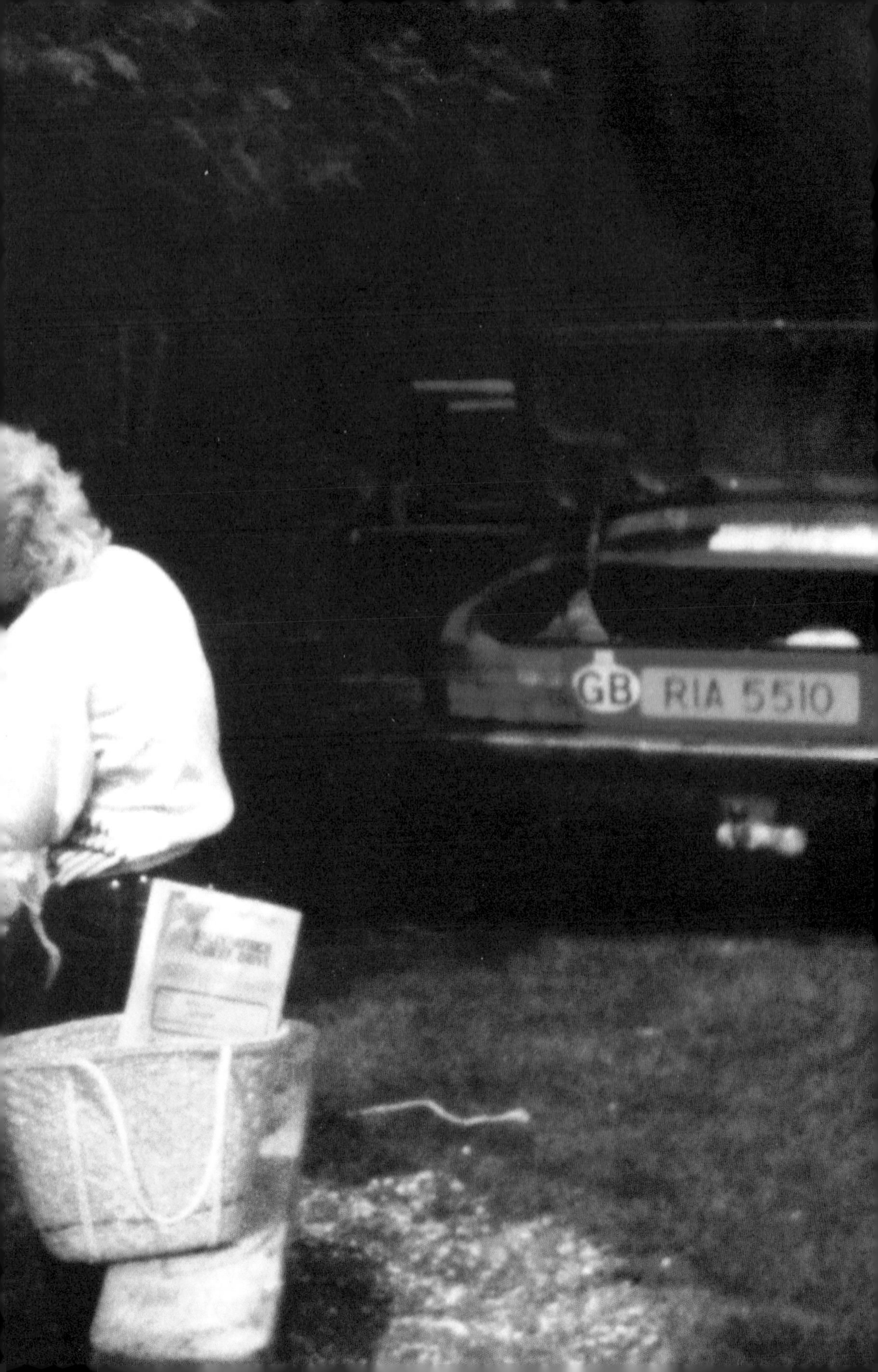
GB
RIA 5510

# THE GOOD STUFF

As a kid it was all about the sweets, crisps and fizzy drinks – some things never change. It's just that then there wasn't the same variety as there is now.

To be fair, when it comes to crisps, Tayto Cheese & Onion were (and are) the favourites and were definitely seen as the healthy option because they contained two veg – potatoes **AND** onions. Who didn't have a cheese and onion crisp sandwich back in the day?

In a way, the nostalgia regarding sweets has been ruined by the fact that a load of companies have recognised we loved those things and brought them out again.

Bar one tiny detail. They've SHRUNK everything. I remember Wham bars being roughly the size of my bedroom door. Mars bars were huge, Snickers were Marathons (Snickers still sounds like knickers to me and I don't care which sporting event they sponsor, it still sounds funny) and Starburst? That just sounds painful. To me they will always be Opal Fruits, made to make your mouth water – you sang that, didn't you?

There were different sweets for mums and dads – the holy grail(s). Like the Fry's Five Centres, Bourneville chocolate, for example, was NOT for kids. Nobody dared take any. That was mums' chocolate.

Wispa bars arrived and changed everything – nobody knew who they were for. They tasted amazing to us kids but they used sexy Gladys and suave Simon from *Hi-de-Hi* whispering to each other in the TV advert.

The adverts were great too! The Milky Bar kid – **AWESOME**. And Milky Bars were awesome. Finger of Fudge and Milky Bar TV ads were also brilliant but these were **NOT COOL** to get! These **DID NOT COUNT** as treats. Milky Way was billed as 'the sweet you can eat between meals without ruining your appetite'. 'A finger of Fudge is just enough to give your kids a treat. A finger of Fudge is just enough until it's time to eat.'

**WHAT?** Fuck that! We **WANTED** our appetite ruined! In our heads this was the first step in the steady downward spiral toward health foods. Sweets you CAN eat? Ridiculous.

Crisps too. We loved crisps. Again, these were categorised by age. Simple crisps – cheese & onion, salt & vinegar, and (at a push, if that's all that was left in the cupboard)

ready salted – were for kids. The more extravagant flavours – prawn cocktail, Worcester sauce, etc. – were for the adults. And then there were the middle-class crisps: your Tudor gammon & pineapples of this world. Another crackin' advert! Every now and then a pretender to Mr Tayto's throne came along – not least Barry McGuigan with his nettle flavour crisps – but nobody has ever **REALLY** displaced the main man* to this day.

Yellow Pack crisps were the guilty secret of the working class. We were no different. 'Please, never **NEVER** put them in my school lunchbox.' I'd often lift the edge of the Tupperware box to check before the unveil. I'd spy some yellow. **YES!!!** Tayto cheese & onion. **WAIT**. Shit no. **ABORT, ABORT!** They're fucking Yellow Pack. The damage had been done. I was a 'packer' – the nickname given to the Yellow Pack massive – for the rest of that term unless, of course, I was able to save myself with a packet of Tudor gammon & pineapple within the week. These were rare though. Often only acquired via a richer friend's house. Jim Megaw and his bloody tasty bargains!

_____

* potato

We used pocket money to buy sweets. Back then finding a ½p equated directly to a Mojo. That's an **ACTUAL** sweet for one half of one penny. Amazing value, and if you **DID** find a ½p (we never called them ha'pennies because that was a granda term), well, it felt like winning the Lottery!*

We never really got into trading cards or sticker books as they were a) too expensive and b) you couldn't eat them. The only time the rule was broken, in our house anyway, was if we qualified for the World Cup! In which case, every penny available went toward stickers. I still remember swapping three Mal Donaghys, a Peter Shilton and **AND** handing over 20p, for a Zico.

I was never into comics, never really 'got them', although my cousin Simon loved them and

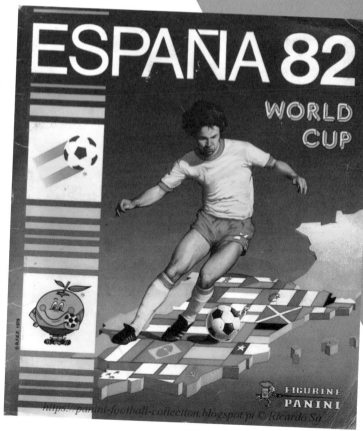

Top – THE most cost-effective way to get sweet treats, the ½p Mojo. Bottom – the hallowed Panini Espana '82 album, which I never did complete.

---

* an assumption since I've never won the Lottery

would be taken in his parents' Mark II Escort to the only shop (that we knew of) in Belfast that sold them. No, the only comics we ever read were the tiniest wee comics that came with ... **THE BAZOOKA JOE!** This was contraband of the highest degree. A class A 'no' from Mum and Dad.

Chewing gum was also off the menu, but bubble gum was top of the hit list. There were a couple of reasons for this. None of us could blow bubbles like they did in the adverts. We all tried, and in fact I'm sure many of us suffered some form of brain injury during our early attempts at simply blowing as hard as we could whilst at the same time not breathing. It was, and remains, a difficult skill. But how could we succeed without practice? This was the first reason parents hated bubblegum. The blow-as-hard-as-you-can-until-your-eyes-are-all-but-popped-out-of-your-head technique. This was bad enough – but you were also always doing it in a group of eager friends who were waiting on 'the bubble'. The problem occurred when – as you used every ounce of strength in your little lungs to fill the not happening bubble – the gum shot out of your mouth like a fucking bullet. Remember in those days, hair was big, hair was everywhere, hair trapped gum.

'**WHAT THE HELL! STEEEEEPHEN!** I'm telling Mum.'

'**NOOOOOOOOOO!** Gavin, don't! Mum will kill me. It's okay! Just wash your hair with soap when we get home.'

The panic and fear were palpable, but I was sure the situation was fixable. Fast forward to my mum coming into the bathroom to find my little brother crying his lamps out, partly due to the fact that his eyes were stinging from a bar of Imperial Leather I'd basically scrubbed his whole head with, and partly because I'd had a cracker idea – to brush it out. Genius. Yeah, that didn't work out so well, so Gavin was now on his hands and knees in the bath, clumps of hair all around him, and not just a lump of bubble gum but also Mum's best hairbrush well and truly wedged close to his scalp.

After getting a skelp and being sent to our room (I was demoted to bottom bunk that night) my mum managed to cut the gum and hairbrush from my brother's hair. As bad as that was, it was the next day I found the most difficult. I had to see him. I had to look him in the eye as we ate our Yellow Pack cornflakes.

This was my only sibling. My brother. My best friend. I loved him. And I'd **DONE THIS** to him. All I could think was ... don't laugh. You know that inner laugh that you know is coming and you can't control? The laugh that only comes when it absolutely and utterly should not? That laugh that starts with gentle suppression which inadvertently leads to mild shoulder shaking?

**DROP THE HEAD, STEPHEN. LOOK SORRIER THAN YOU EVER HAVE.** Whatever you do, **DO NOT LOOK AT YOUR BROTHER'S HACK-JOB HAIRDO** (*shoulders start*). But I concentrate and try to think of serious stuff whilst staring at the bowl. Okay. Remember the time that rabbit died after running out in front of the Vauxhall Viva? That's good. I loved that rabbit. Granda was raging, though, that it had dented the chrome bumper. Hang on. (*Shoulders are away again.*) Oh come on. That's not even remotely funny.

But you know once **THAT** laugh starts, basically, you're screwed.

Okay, I think I'm getting away with it. Silence bar the clinking of spoons on cereal bowls.

I'm getting calmer. I can do this. Just as long as I don't glance up and catch a glimpse of that sad wee face with that weird crazy skinhead-bouffant hybrid, I might just make it.

I could feel Mum's fury through her eyes, which were boring into the top of my head.

'Are you laughing, Stephen? Do you think this is funny?'

Perfect. The tone scared me so much, the laughter had gone. I had discovered the antidote. Or so I thought.

'Look at him.'

'What? (*Munching faster on the cornflakes now.*) No.'

'Sorry, what did you say to me?' Ahhhhhhhh ...

**'LOOK AT YOUR BROTHER.'**

And that was that. As I raised my eyes, I bypassed sniggering and moved straight to convulsing with laughter, tears tripping me ... The rest was a blur of loud voices, crying and the sole of a slipper.

I didn't eat gum again until I was in my late teens.

# FAST (ish) FOOD (ish)

Eating out back in the day was strictly for special occasions. And there were not the choices that there are today. Very occasionally we got a chippy from the chippy. Sausages, burgers, pasties, fish, or onion rings … with chips. That was the choice.

And it didn't matter which one of these deep-fried, heart-attack-inducing greasy morsels you consumed, if someone asked you what you'd had the night before, you answered, 'We had a chippy.'

Chippies were everywhere and they were nearly all independently owned. There were no McDonalds or KFCs back in the day. But for a while, just opposite the City Hall in Belfast, there was a Wimpy Burger. This was like walking on to the set of *Happy Days*. It was as close as many of us had ever been and would ever get, to the USA. Bright lights and red seats and music, and American pictures everywhere! We felt that we WERE in America. Well, right up to the point when you

ordered, and some angry teenager barked, 'What's yours, love?' Not how they did it on *Cagney & Lacey*, but we ignored the accent and kept up the pretence that we had just walked in off Times Square.

'Can I have a Big Mac, please?'

'Does this look like a fuckin' McDonalds, ya wee shite? Away on da fuck.'

Time for a rethink.

'What do you have?'

(We asked these questions, by the way, in probably the worst American accents you've ever heard.)

'Are those fuckin' eyes painted on, son? Look at the board.'

She nodded her head behind, to where there was a photograph of

THE most amazing succulent cheese burger, like nothing I'd ever seen before.

'I'll have one of them, ma'am.'

'That'll be thee fifty.'

Three pounds fifty. What the fuck? I only had a fiver with me and had anticipated that it would get me a can of Lilt and a packet of Barry McGuigan's nettle crisps for the train home (and the train fare, although I had planned to fall asleep when the conductor came round).

But I was in this far. Now I knew how Mum felt at the Woolworth's counter. 'Aye. I mean, yes please, ma'am. I'll take your best cheeseburger.'

'No prablim,' she grunted. I was sure I could hear her mumble something along the lines of 'fuckin' wee culchie dicks coming here acting like the fuckin' Waltons' but I couldn't be sure. Lawrence, Gavin and I were the epitome of provincial sophistication so I'm sure I imagined it.

I waited approximately thirty seconds before being handed a polystyrene box with my dream burger lying within. I thanked the pleasant girl and took my treasure upstairs. Blinded by smoke from older teenagers and old men, we found a table and sat down. The excitement levels were astronomical.

'A real American burger.'

'I know.'

We opened the boxes (they squeaked the way polystyrene does when you rub it together and we shuddered as one). Anyway as we opened the box, what greeted us was just about as far away from the photo we'd been directed to as was possible. A dry bread roll with a cheese slice and a limp burger that was giving the cheese slice a run for its money in a 'Who's thinnest?' competition. There was already red sauce on it (fancy) and it was lukewarm. It was, I am fairly sure, completely disgusting and borderline poisonous, but to us, it was the **REAL** taste of America and you couldn't wipe the smile off our wee ketchup*-soaked faces.

---

\* Ketchup was a term that was introduced via American television as it became more popular. In our day it was red sauce. If you'd asked for ketchup, you'd either have been greeted by 'Wha?' or 'Get da fuck, ya posh wee dick.'

# EXOTIC(ish) FOOD

**Fast food was a luxury back then. Exotic was Chinese food. Chinese food was chicken fried rice (if you were a child) or beef chow mein with noodles if you were a grown-up.**

This was the height of sophistication in our house and was something very special indeed. I'm not saying that Chinese restaurants didn't have a fairly substantial menu with all sorts of exotic-sounding foods: they absolutely did. The thing was, when my dad had made the fairly big decision that we were 'having a Chinese', there was no room for failure. Keep your Peking Ducks and Thai-style Kung Po chickens. My dad liked what he liked, and when he found something he liked, he stuck to it. One thing he didn't like was talking to strangers.

Never mind foreign strangers. So there was no way he was ever going to experiment with the menu.

We never complained too much though, to be fair. My brother and I loved (and still love) chicken fried rice. Plus, as we got older, we became more aware of our parents, like all children do, and we desperately didn't ever want to witness ever again anything like the conversation our dad had with the owner of the Chi Koo in Carrickfergus in 1984.

'Right, boys, let's go for something a bit different tonight. What do you say?'

Chi Koo in all its glory (this was it at its peak). Also, the scene of the worst accent crime never recorded.

'YEEEESSSS. Let's try it! It'll be delicious, Dad!'

The three of us jump into the Ford Orion while Mum gets the table ready. 'Get us something nice,' she says as we leave.

'Don't worry, Mum. We will!'

We are starving and excited. Just going into the Chinese was like walking into a different world. There were always pictures on the walls that were sort of 3-D velour scenarios showing dragons and wild beasts and beautiful girls with tiny wee lips. The pictures were practically begging to be touched. Every time we went in, though, we got the all-too-familiar 'don't youse touch a fuckin' thing in here' whispered with force through a grimace that turned to a smile as the owner made his way to the till.

'Harro. We like to try eat some new Chinese food. You tell us which one best.'

Hang on. What?

I glanced at Gavin who was looking at me quizzically. I was the older brother so he assumed I knew what was going down. I had no clue. All I knew was that my dad's grasp of

English was suddenly minimal, and the few sentences he did know were coming out in a horrendously awful Chinese accent. This was back in the day before political correctness became part of our thinking but even then I knew something wasn't right.

'Sorry, sir. What are you asking me?' replied Martin, the owner of the Chi Koo Chinese takeaway near our house, a man we became good friends with over the years, a kind man, a smart man, a man who spoke PERFECT English.

'We like try new Chinese food, prease.'

OH.

MY.

GOD.

Please make this stop. Gavin looked at me again. He looked like he might cry. I knew how he felt.

'What type of food do you like, sir?' Again, perfect English.

'We like flied lice, and we also like eat chicken and beef wif nooda. But none that aul fancy Kung Po ballix. You have difflent chicken and normaa beef?'

Seriously? I start reading the Chinese calendar. It's in Chinese but I need a distraction.

'Well, sir. Let me see if I can work out what you're after and see if we can't find something that you'll find appetizing.'

'That sound velly good.'

As Dad and Martin continued their frankly disturbing conversation, Gavin and I were cooling down with a wee Chinese fan that Martin's wife had given us to play with. It was obvious her maternal instincts had kicked in. She recognised two young boys who had obviously experienced some sort of shock to their little systems.

When we arrived back at the house with our white bags filled with tinfoil bowls, plastic straws and as many soy sauce sachets as we could steal, Mum could see something was wrong.

'What's wrong, boys? Youse okay?'

I glanced at Gavin again. We nodded that nod that only siblings have. The nod that indicated that what we had just witnessed was never to be talked about again. Ever.

'No, nothing. Just hungry.'

I lied and told the truth in equal measure.

'Well? What did we get?'

'Two beef chow mein and a chicken fried rice for the boys to share,' said Dad.

'Ach lovely,' said Mum.

# THE SKANDIA

Then there was 'eating out'. Like proper EATING OUT. These days, people eat out all the time. The choices now are phenomenal. Belfast alone has some of the finest chefs and dining experiences in the world, for crying out loud!

That wasn't always the case however. As we got a little older we would venture to the new trendy eateries that had opened up, you know, the Chicago Pizza Pie Factories of this world. Kids' birthday parties by day; Hooch-fuelled shenanigans by night. Never a final destination, but a stop-off on the way to the Crescent.

As a kid, though, eating out was a big deal and one that was ONLY ever to celebrate a special occasion. A birthday, an 11+ pass, getting your

**Birthday parties included a bottle of lemonade and mini sausages on sticks as standard. Sandwiches and birthday cakes were ALWAYS home-made and tasted unreal!**

driving licence – you know, that sort of thing. It was a **LUXURY!** And for us, there was only one place ... The Skandia. I think the correct name was simply Skandia but we knew it as **THE** Skandia. It was **THE** place of choice for our family. When I try to remember, it seems as though Nana Reilly was always the instigator of these outings. Once we knew we were going, the excitement levels were second to none. We knew exactly what was happening when Mum uttered the immortal words, 'Go and put your brown cord suits on. Your nana is taking you to town.'

**YES!!** Game on!

We always took the train. It only went as far as York Street station and then there was a connecting bus that took you on into town. The trains were minging. The hard seats were difficult to get purchase on (even in brown corduroy trousers) and quite often I'd slowly slide forward until my back was on the seat, my neck at an unnatural angle against the seat back, and my knees buried in the crotch of some poor random person sitting across from me.

The hard seats were always the better choice, though. Yes, at first

There are no twenty-first century printers in the world that can do the burnt orange and brown exterior justice, so we made this photo black and white.

glance those comfy, brown-and-orange soft seats looked preferable but there was one major flaw in their design. They were absorbent. Like sponge. Even during the summer when they'd 'dried out', sitting on them released a cloud of stale smoke, urine and vomit that, these days, would be classed as a chemical attack. Brutal. So, it was the hard seats for us.

One of the other things about the trains back then was the doors. They had no handles on the inside. Only the outside. Which meant that the ONLY way to open the carriage and let yourself out was to pull the window down (with some degree of force, if I remember correctly) and stick your head out. That's all well and good (actually, not even really that good) when the vehicle is stationary, but we all did it when the train was moving. Not because we had a death wish, but because of the fear of missing our stop. If you didn't get that window down, and the conductor didn't see you, you could be stuck. And then you'd have to try and get back to your original stop without paying by explaining that you'd got stuck. That didn't wash with Northern Ireland Railways staff. Plus, and this was key, EVERYWHERE in town closed at 9-ish. And when I say closed, I mean, closed! So, if our trip to THE Skandia meant my wee Nana Reilly had to stick her head out of a 200-ton moving vehicle at 45 mph then, by fuck, the head was out.

Arriving at York Street, it was then a short wait for the bus, Gavin and I in our best 'Sunday outfit' (every kid had a Sunday outfit, primarily for Sunday School, but it doubled up for special occasions like this one) and Nana in her best outfit, complete with hair freshly permed, smelling deliciously of lilac and Shah biscuits. (She loved to bake and when Gavin and I were visiting she made our favourite aforementioned biscuits. Even smelling anything remotely similar now takes me straight back.)

The bus had a similar seat situation to the train so again we took the hard seats. Our train ticket got us into the centre of Belfast. I remember on one particular occasion we were redirected because a bomb had taken out the windows in the old Co-Op building (it was called 'The Co' by everyone in NI) but this just seemed normal to us. We arrived at the city limits. This was the 'exclusion zone' where all normal cars had to stop. There was no access to the city for non-military vehicles, not because we all wanted a lovely pedestrianised area, conducive to entertainment and shopping, but because non-military vehicles had an awful habit of exploding if they did get in!

At the security gate the bus stopped and the 'hut man' got on. He carried what was essentially a cross between a golf club and a hand mirror – the mirror at the bottom of the club, at an angle, so he could see under the seats. I remember years later a friend of mine came over from Scotland and we took him into town. At the hut, he asked what the hut man was doing. 'Checking for bombs,' said Gavin in the matter-of-fact way we all had, not knowing any different.

'WHAT DA FUCK? Checkin fir BOMBS! And wha dae FUCK do we do if he fuckin finds one?!'

'We either exit the bus en masse, calmly in single file, or we all leave together through the windows at about 120 mph.'

The dark sense of humour back again.

This didn't settle him at all, strangely enough.

A common sight in Northern Ireland back in the day. Note the people just getting on with things ... probably rushing to the bomb damage sale.

With Nana, we headed straight round to the Skandia. We wanted desperately to go to Leisureworld but knew better than to ask. We were already in the middle of a treat and asking for more was **NOT** an option. Nana Reilly was one of the sweetest and most beautiful women I've ever met, but like all women of that era who endured so much, she was quite, quite formidable when she needed to be. So upon arriving at the Skandia, it was best behaviour all round from Gavin and me. There was promise of a dessert if we didn't mess about, and that was enough carrot. We didn't dare go down the stick road with Nana.

The first big decision was what to order. Now, on the odd occasion that Dad took us out, he looked at menus in a way that only men know how to. It's still the same to this day. Many men look at a menu the complete opposite way to women. Yes, we thank the staff. Yes, we smile across the table at whoever we are with. Yes, we admire the scenery, the ambiance, the smells emanating from the kitchen. And yes, we hold the menu up and draw our finger slowly down all the options, same as women, bar one small thing …

Women are moving their fingers down over each meal, wondering which will go best with which wine. Men LOOK like they are doing the same but we have no idea what the food is, we are just slowly drawing our fingers down the prices of the dishes.

Our inner dialogue goes along these lines:

That's okay.

Not bad.

Balls. They were starters I was looking at.

What the fuck are they making the batter from?!

If that doesn't come with free chips I'm making a fucking complaint.

Hope she had a big lunch.

If she chooses the lobster, I'm doing a fucking runner, and so on …

I, of course, have never done this.*

Anyway, back to The Skandia.

---

* cough

It didn't matter what we had – it was probably fish and chips with copious amounts of red sauce. Maybe fish fingers straight out of the supermarket, but dolled up for The Skandia with a sprig of who-knows-what. Whatever it was, we loved it. But it was Nana's dinner that I remember most vividly.

'What are youse havin', love?'

'The boys will have fish fingers, chips and bayns –' the posh accent was brought out especially for The Skandia – 'and I will be having Chicken Maryland.'

CHICKEN MARYLAND! The poshest of all dinners available in Northern Ireland until 10 April 1998, when it was agreed by all parties as part of the Good Friday Agreement that other fancy dishes would be made available too.

Chicken Maryland! Even the words bring back memories of chicken, banana fritters, meats, sausages, chicken, pineapple ring fritters, chicken and more chicken! I can't even remember what else was on that gargantuan plate, but there was a LOT of it, and there was no rhyme nor reason to any of it. Meat, vegetables, fruit, more meat, boiled stuff, fried stuff, deep-fried stuff, and chicken.

LOTS and lots of chicken. I remember as a child thinking I would, ONE DAY, order my very own Chicken Maryland, but by the time I grew up and was eating out, the chicken remained, but the mystical state of Maryland had been replaced by the not-so-mystical state of Kentucky.

Older people too always ordered a 'wee bit of piccalilli' to go with their meal. Fluorescent yellow, vinegar-soaked vegetables that looked to all intents and purposes like a specimen jar from a biology class. It's still available to this day, but I've yet to see anyone under fifty-five buying it. It won't be that long until I too am part of the piccalilli massive.

Dessert was the best part and there was only ever one option, IF we had been good, and IF we were allowed. The advert that ran on TV showed a family with some sort of triangular cake-knife thing cutting through it, the crackling of the chocolate making us salivate every time. It was, of course, Viennetta! Now THIS was what it felt like to be rich. This was how the other half rolled! This was THE SKANDIA!! Nana ALWAYS had a pot of tea with hers and we either had Coca Cola if we were heading back to our own house or water if we were heading back to Nana's. (I never understood the logic of this until I had my own children … Fizzy drinks and kids do not make for a calm evening in front of the fire, but if you are dropping them off with someone else, fizzy drinks are grand!)

Everything was paid for in cash in those days, so Nana got her ENORMOUS purse out and paid the lady, left a tip, and off we went, back to the bus stop to retrace our steps home.

---

**10% SERVICE ADDED TO ALL CHARGES**

**Appetisers**
1. NORWEGIAN PRAWN COCKTAIL ... 6/-
2. Chilled Grapefruit Cocktail ... 2/-
3. CRAB COCKTAIL ... 5/-
4. BEST HOME PRODUCED SMOKED SALMON ... 7/6
5. EGG MAYONNAISE
6. MELON RING Half with Tingling Water Ice ... 5/-
7. SKANDIA HORS D'OEUVRE ... 3/9
8. Frosted Fruit Juices: Pure Orange, Grapefruit or Tomato ... 7/-
9. DANISH CAVIAR on SMOKED SALMON ... 8/6

**Soups** with Roll and Butter
11. Rich Tomato with Dairy Cream ...
12. SWEDISH STYLE GOLDEN PEA & HAM ... 1/10
13. Dairy Cream of Chicken ... 1/10
14. FRENCH STYLE ONION SOUP ... 1/10 / 3/6

**Cold Specialities of the House**
21. Fashion Fruit Plate: Diced Fruit, Carrot and Cheese Salad 5/6
22. GOLDEN GULF SALAD: Prawns, Crab & Smoked Salmon 10/-
23. Roast Ham & Pineapple: Cottage Cheese & Russian Salad 10/-
24. VIKING Treasure Bowl: Filled with Cold Meat & Seafoods 7/6
25. ROAST LEG of PORK with Apple & Celery Salad 11/6
26. TONGUE with EGG MAYONNAISE 6/6
27. Salmon with Russian, Beetroot & Apple Salad 6/6
28. BREAST of CHICKEN & HAM: Apple & Celery Salad 9/6
29. Caribbean Salad: Assorted Fruits, Carrot, Cheeses & Nuts 7/6

**Hot Specialities of the House**
30. Escalope of Veal Garnished with Fr. Egg & Vegetables 10/6
31. Mini-Chicken Grill with Bacon, Mushrooms & Fr. Fried Potatoes
32. FRIED SCAMPI, Lemon and French Fried Potatoes 6/9
33. Roast Breast of Chicken & Ham with Peas, & Roast Potatoes 9/6
34. Duckling A L'Orange with Peas & Duchesse Potatoes 14/-
35. Fried Fillet of Plaice, Lemon and French Fried Potatoes 14/-
36. Fillets of Lemon Sole Bonne Femme and New Potatoes 6/-
37. Fried Chicken Maryland and Croquette Potatoes 9/-
38. North Sea Platter: Fried Sea Gems, Scampi & Fried Potatoes 7/-
39. Curried Leg of Chicken with Peas & Patna Rice 7/6

**Char-Grill:** MAGIC OPEN HEARTH FOR SUCCULENT STEAKS and CHOPS
41. Mini-Steak: Tomato and French Fried Potatoes
42. Fillet Steak (6 oz.) ,,
43. ,, (8 oz.) ,, 6/9
44. Sirloin Steak (6 oz.) ,, 14/6
45. ,, ,, 17/6
46. Pork Chop, Pineapple, Peas & Fr. Fried Potatoes 11/6
47. Lamb Cutlets (2) 13/-
48. Mixed Grill (Cutlet, Chipolata, Bacon, Steak, Tomato, Egg and French Fried Potatoes) 8/-
49. Pork Fillet Garnished with Pineapple, Peas & Fr. Fried Potatoes 11/6

**Vegetables**
Roast, Duchesse or Croquette Potatoes 9/-
Peas, French Beans, Button Sprouts, Mushrooms 2/-
French Fried Onions or Cauliflower 1/6 / 2/6

**Salad Bowls**
51. Lettuce and Tomato Salad with French Dressing 2/6
52. Garden Salad: Lettuce, Tomato, Egg and Cucumber 3/6
53. Apple and Celery on Lettuce 2/-

**Eggs and Omelettes**
61. Bacon, Egg & Sausage with Fr. Fried Potatoes
62. Bacon, Sausage & Tomato with Fr. Fried Potatoes 6/-
63. Omelettes: Plain, Cheese, Prawn, Mushroom or Ham 6/-
64. Scrambled Eggs with Prawns, Bacon or Ham 6/6
65. Bacon or Sausages with Fr. Fried Potatoes 5/-

**Smorrebrod:** Danish Open Sand...
71. INTERNATIONAL: Irish Ham with
72. GOURMET: Smoked Salmon & Norw...
73. DANES DELIGHT: Pork, Apple and
74. CONTINENTAL: Danish Salami...
75. TIVOLI: Egg Mayonnaise with Danis...
76. GANGPLANK: Ham, Pork, Cheeses an...
77. CRAB NEW ORLEANS: Crab, Cocktail...
78. FJORD CATCH
79. SKANDIA: Chicken Drumstick and Ham...

**Toasted Sandwich Specialit...**
(from 10 a.m.—10 p.m.
81. Cheese, Ham & Pineapple with Savory...
82. Ham and Cheese with Pickle
83. Skandia Club Triple Deck: Breast of Chic...
84. Prawns and Creamed Cheese...
85.

**Continental Ice Creams**
91. Vacherin Slice: Dairy Ice Cream, Raspberr... and Meringue
92. Mela Stregata: Strega Flavoured Ice Cream in...
93. Praline: Nutty Flavoured Mixed with Almond T...
94. Swedish Style with Dairy Cream...
95. MARSALA Gateau with Fruit Salad...
96. Butterscotch Sundae

**Dessert Specialities**
101. Apple Pie with Dairy Cream or Swedish Style Ic...
102. PAVLOVA with Strawberries
103. Skandia Trifle
104. White Peaches and Dairy Cream...
105. Fruit Salad with Dairy Cream or Swedish Style P...
106. Hot Pineapple Fritters with Dairy Cream...
107. Greek Baldji Figs and Dairy Cream...
108. Rum Baba, Fruit Salad and Cream

**Cheeses** with Biscuits
111. Cheddar, Bel Paese, Danish Blue, Brie, Camembe... Suisse
112. YOGHURT: Assorted Fruit Flavours...

**Patisserie**
121. Pastries
122. Danish Pastry
123. Gateau or Flan

**Beverages**
131. CHILLED CONTINENTAL APPLE JUICE...
132. Chilled Peach Nectar...
133. CHILLED RED or WHITE GRAPE JUICE...
134. Ice Cool Milk
135. Frosted Orange, Coca-Cola or Lemon...
136. CHILLED YMER: Scandinavian Style Cultered Milk G...
137. SKANDIA Style Coffee with Cream...
138. SKANDIA Style Coffee with Cream Separately...
139. CEYLON De Luxe Tea
140. RUSSIAN Tea with Lemon...

# NANA'S HOUSE

Arriving home to Nana's was something else I loved. The house was always pitch black and always freezing. She had no central heating as we know it today, and instead all heat originated from the open fire in the living room and the one in the bedroom. Now a fire in the bedroom sounds quite posh, but Nana lived in a very modest terraced house and this was standard.

Once we got in and turned on the lights (there was electricity; I'm not quite that old) we kept our duffle coats on and sat in the living room, expertly wrapped in a blanket, waiting. Waiting on the lighting of the fire!

This was almost like a form of modern interpretative dance in its beautifully poetic precision. Nana had usually cleared the fireplace for our return and so it was sitting – cleaned, empty, ready. All of the tools required hung by the fire on a kind of wrought iron, multi-hooked hanging thing, like a miniature version of a garden set in many ways. A little tiny brush, a pitchfork-type thing and a little spade were the weapons of choice. Next to that, was the poker (always bigger and always placed next to the hearth, both because of its size and also as a reminder that it could be used as a form of punishment ... it never was but the threat was there and that was enough), firelighters (Sunny Jim) a small bucket of wood, a coal bucket and the pièce de résistance – last night's *Belfast Tele*. It was this last bit that always intrigued us.

The paper back then was enormous and all but covered Nana, yet whilst asking us if we enjoyed the Skandia, and if we wanted a Shah biscuit and some milk for supper, she did something that I have never seen done since. She seemed to roll up the paper, flatten the roll, twist the ends and fold it up like some sort of origami ninja. She then dropped into the fire what looked to us like a weird, snake-like creature. And this was repeated maybe five or six times in the space of literally ninety seconds. A hearth full of *Belfast Telegraph* snakes. These were the foundations for the fire.

Sticks were added next, then coal – **NOT TOO MUCH!** – just enough to 'get her lit'.

Within minutes of arriving at the dark, freezing cold house, this wizard of a woman transformed the living room into the cosiest place on the planet.

Shah biscuit in one hand, cup of warm milk with honey in the other, I'm not sure if that type of genuine feeling of being in a proper **HOME** – that warmth, not just from the blazing fire, but from my nana and her house, will never, or could ever, be recreated or felt again.

Sweets For My Sweet, C.J. Lewis
Eye of the Tiger, Survivor
Jack & Diane, John Mellencamp
Keep on Movin', Soul II Soul
Town Called Malice, The Jam
Do You Really Want To Hurt Me, Culture Club
When Yer Man Gets the Ball, Dana & the 1982 Northern Ireland
World Cup Squad (might be difficult to get this one, LOL!)
Stand and Deliver, Adam & the Ants
A Good Heart, Feargal Sharkey
Happy Days theme
Kung Fu Fighting, Carl Douglas

**EATING MIX TAPE**

The Clements men completely engrossed in the Northern Ireland v Brazil match at Mexico '86 at the Eglinton Hotel in Portrush.

# Chapter Five

# ...AND DRINKING

As you got older and started drinking, a whole new world opened up. Growing up and being quite sporty, I was never that into drinking or getting drunk. Our parents were fairly liberal with both my brother and me. The general rule was 'So long as you don't get drunk, and we know where you are, that's fine.'

We took them up on this offer with varying degrees of success. As far as lagers went (and they weren't called lagers, it was beer) we had a few options. If we were feeling flush, and the offies stocked it, then Budweiser or Miller Genuine Draught were always desirable. As well as probably

Pretending to be drunk whilst wearing a skinny pea-green leather tie and diamond cardigan, and holding a glass of white Shloer. Like an early Val Doonican.

being relatively good quality, they also made us look the part – you know, like modern Danny Zukos. But without the woman. Or car. And wearing a pale blue shellsuit. Okay. We looked fuck-all like any American movie star but we THOUGHT we must look the part because we were drinking the can!

After that, there was our local Harp – 'Give us a pint a Harp and a packet of dates, please' on repeat from all your mates when you were drinking it, which seemed as funny the hundredth time as the first. One of the few benefits of drinking.

LCL Pils and Colt 45 were also brands I remember. Colt 45 was like a shit Budweiser, and LCL was always a hit with the girls, if we ever were in the company of any, because someone somewhere had stated that LCL stood for low calorie lager, and, as often happens with schoolyard rumour, it became fact.

Our favourite beer, and bear in mind that to young drinkers like us, they all tasted horrible (we drank more for the effects than for pleasure), was Tennent's Lager. Because it was made with real Scottish hops and yeast and barley and spring water forced through a

crack in the mountains which filtered it to give a clean, fresh, malty taste.

Nah, mate, it was because there was a picture of Sandra on the side of the tin with her baps being restrained by a doily masquerading as a bra. Sexism in its most outrageous form. It was, and still is, unbelievable that these things existed.

Back then, I didn't know what sexism was. I didn't know what sex was, for crying out loud! There was no internet, 'magazines' were not commonplace, and so this was the closest most of us had been to a naked or semi-naked woman. (Sadly, this also remained the closest we would get to a naked or semi-naked woman for many, many years.)

Looking back now it's ridiculous, but I remember two mates getting into an actual fist fight, because Paul accused Lawrence of taking his Linda.

'I had two Bettys, a Sandra and a Deirdre. If I'd had your Linda too I wouldn't be able to speak, for fuck's sake!'

'Well, someone's necked a Linda of mine and left me a half-finished, lukewarm Shirley.'

*[Fight breaks out for 45 seconds before everyone falls down laughing, and drunk.]*

I often wondered, though, what a passing tourist* would have made of the conversation if they'd overheard it.

Cider was different too. It's a kind of trendy drink these days but back then it was Olde English or Strongbow, it was in a plastic bottle, and the bottle was BIG. Two litres was the absolute minimum amount that you could take out in public. One litre bottles were strictly for girls ... This was often the drink of choice as we foolishly told each other that 'Yer ma won't smell anything bar apples, so make it past the living room and up the stairs without falling, slurring, boking or crying, and all she will smell will be the faint whiff of a Granny Smith.'

Of course this was not (and is not) the case. For a start, we always came home with a mouthful of Polo mints. Because Polo mints made your breath smell fresh, like mint, in fact. There were a few problems with the Polo

_____

* Not that there were any tourists back then. Well, certainly very few, and should they have happened upon us, I'm sure they would have had some story to relay to their friends back home. 'We went to Northern Ireland and they even fight over the percentage of women consumed.'

solution, though. One: it was thought that the best way to get the most out of them was to pack as many into your mouth as was humanly possible. This had its own problem. You see, because they had holes in them, speaking would often end up becoming very difficult. Long before every rubbish impressionist was doing the late Ian Paisley, we were sounding like him, simply because we whistled through the holes as we talked.

The other problem was something we all should have been aware of. We had all brushed our teeth. We had all eaten apples. So we should have known that the mint/apple combo was not a pleasant one. And given that we already had the guts of two litres of fermented apple juice in our bodies, the one thing we didn't need was a foodstuff that would trigger retching.

'If you can make it past the living room without falling, slurring, boking or crying ...'

Remember those words.

The problem was, we often managed all those things within about sixty seconds of clattering through the door.

'Hi Mum,' I mumbled. Right, straight upstairs, bathroom, and bed.

'Good night son?'

**SHIT!**

I can't say no – she'll want to know why. But I can't say yes because I've a mouthful of fucking Polo mints,

Red Red Wine, UB40
Making Your Mind Up, Bucks Fizz
Sledgehammer, Peter Gabriel
Walk Like an Egyptian, The Bangles
Papa Don't Preach, Madonna
Take My Breath Away, Berlin
Danger Zone, Kenny Loggins
Word Up, Cameo
Take Me Home Tonight, Eddie Money
Nasty, Janet Jackson

DRINKING MIX TAPE

and it'll come out YESSSSSSSS, and that's not all that'll come out because I can't get rid of the saliva in my mouth because the holes in the Polos are acting as some sort of spittle reservoir.

'Not bad.'

No Ss in that one. Okay, some mint spit dribbled onto my ABIDAS sweatshirt, but I'll say it was a bird or something in the morning.

'Okay son, night night then.'

**YESSSSHHHHH!**

I'd made it to the bathroom.

I considered not brushing my teeth. I mean, how much mint flavour can a fella take? But thought better of it. I crunched the Polos away and set about brushing my teeth. Now, on the way home, I'd stopped at Martin's Chi Koo. I've been to some amazing restaurants as an adult. Some top-class Michelin-starred joints. Meals that have cost almost as much as my first car, for fuck's sake, yet nothing I've ever tasted since, tasted as **GOOOOOOD** as a fried rice and chips, with gravy, garden peas and onions – Chi Koo's stunning 'gravy half-and-half' after two litres of Olde E and a half-tin of Sandra.

Experience is a great teacher. As you get older, you learn certain things about going out.

You learn when to start drinking for an evening; you learn (hopefully) when to stop. You learn that a glass of water before bed cures nothing, but will make you need to go to the toilet in the middle of the night. You also learn that there is a point in your mouth, and it's different for every individual, but there IS a point beyond which, if you've been drinking, the toothbrush must not go. No, this is not the best in oral hygiene, but you learn that those couple of back teeth will take one for the team, and in any case, they'll get an extra special brushing in the morning.

I was young though. And hadn't learned. And attacked my teeth like a man possessed. My hand was going like a piston. (If you've just picked up the book in a shop and happened upon this last sentence, please, **PLEASE**, go back and read at least a few sentences before too.) Anyway, back to the teeth. I was merrily brushing away, congratulating myself on a successful night of getting 'blakked' and getting away with it, when suddenly I felt it. It was just a small twinge in my tummy area to begin with. I stopped and cocked my head. 'What was that?' I thought to myself. I waited a bit ... Nah, nothing.

Michael, my Dutch friend, and I posing with a bear. We had so many good times. Michael and I, not the teddy.

I continued brushing with all the vigour and enthusiasm that had been taught us by our parents and the Colgate ads.

Wait! There it was again. Only stronger. I glanced in the mirror. It happened again, but this time I noticed that my jaw opened up full. But I didn't open my mouth, I thought to myself. The tummy muscles contractions coupled with the involuntary mouth opening became more regular. I wondered if this was what it was like to give birth.

The time between contractions was shortening. The involuntary jaw opening was now accompanied by a kind of a death-gasp type noise. Like pushing the last breath out of your lungs, but then stopping dramatically. I looked at myself in the mirror again.

WHO THE FUCK WAS THIS!?!?!

The sight of the fella looking back at me scared the shit out of me! Some puffy-faced, bloodshot-eyed, green bloke who was sweating profusely. I almost called for Mum, until I realised that I was looking at my own reflection. This was an unexpected and not entirely welcome development. You have this. You can control this, I thought to myself. I thought wrong. I knew what NOT to think about anyway. Not to think about lukewarm fermented apples, with Sandra chasers, a mouthful of mints and a gravy half-and-half, that if I remembered correctly had begun to cool down and as it did, didn't the fat start to congeal on top of the …

BAAAAAAAAAAAAZZZZZZZZ-ZZZZAAAAAAAAAAAHHHHHHHH-HHHH!!!!!

NOOOOOO.

I wasn't being sick. I was vomiting. There is a massive difference.

When people are sick they almost politely regurgitate something in their tummy that hasn't agreed with them. Until there is no more, and then they take some fluids, and end the process of being sick.

No. I was not being sick. I was vomiting. I had zero control. I was gone. Away with it.

Have you ever seen someone watering their garden with a high pressure hose? I'm sure you have. Now, have you ever seen that person let go of the hose so that it flails about wildly, spraying water everywhere? I was the out-of-control hose.

BAAAAAAAAAAAAZZZZZZZZZ-ZAAAAAAHHHHHHHHHHHHHH!!!!!

Fuck me! What the hell am I going to do?

Man has searched since the beginning of time for perpetual motion – something which, once activated, will run for ever. It is, of course, impossible as it would violate the first or second law of thermodynamics. But that night, I believed I was living proof that perpetual motion was possible. I was sick. I stopped. I thought about what I had eaten. I was sick again. I was sick. I stopped. I thought about what I had drank. I was sick again.

Perpetual motion.

Fuck your laws of thermodynamics, I was breaking the law. I was smashing that law to bits. Problem was I was also smashing a bottle of Dad's Brut 33. The force of my crushed-Polo-laced sick (it was like sand blasting, for fuck's sake) had knocked it off the shelf. I was in trouble. I didn't care. I just wanted it

A deadly weapon used on the dating scene. It was said women couldn't resist, although I did a good job of proving the marketing people wrong.

to stop. My neck was getting sore as it thrashed about from the force of the vomiting; my stomach muscles were like an Olympic boxer's from pumping this shit up.

'Stephen! Are you okay up there?'

Mum.

Fuck.

I can't open my mouth to reply. I'm trying to fight the stomach muscles propelling the vomit by holding my hand over my mouth. Another rookie error.

**PPFFFFFFFFFFFSHHH- HAAAAAAKKAAKKKAAAA!**

Awesome. You know when someone's watering their garden and they turn the knob at the end of the hose from jet to spray? That. Maximum coverage.

I could hear Mum coming up the stairs. I was too tired to care. I was a beaten man–boy. I had no energy left in me. No fight.

Mum burst into the bathroom to a scene of absolute carnage.

Years later I watched *The Exorcist* and there is a scene in that movie not unlike what my poor mum walked into (without the religious significance).

'Stephen! Look at the bathroom! Are you okay?'

I glanced up through bleary bloodshot eyes, with Chi-Koo dripping from my nose, looking around me at the newly Polo-pebble-dashed mirrors in the bathroom. 'Mmmmuuuuhhhh, fine Mum. What's up?'

I gave a few shudders. A couple of gravy cider bubbles appeared.

I was done.

It was over.

'Awwwwwk son. Look at the hack of you. Are you sure you are okay?'

'Yes Mum. I'm fine. Must've been something I ate.'

'Don't you give me that you wee ...'

And that was the last thing I heard.

I was skelped.

Mum never did tell my dad about the incident, and to this day there is not a single shred of evidence it even occurred, bar one tiny wee nick on the floor tiles where a bottle of Brut 33 was blasted off its shelf by a cannon of cider, Sandra, gravy half-and-half and Polo mints.

As a postscript to this story, and to give you an insight into how crap I was at learning from mistakes, the only thing I **NEVER** touched again from the offending concoction was ...

... Polo mints.

# Chapter Six

# SCHOOL

'The best days of your life.' That's what all the grown-ups used to say. I remember vividly sitting in the sixth-year common room (actually just a classroom with no teacher present) and saying to my best mate Steenson, 'If these are the best years of our lives, I'm not looking forward to the rest because this is shit.' Looking back, they now do seem like some of the best years ... I wouldn't say THE best, but certainly not the worst either.

# PRIMARY SCHOOL

Being a dad to a school-age daughter, I have a little window into what schools are like these days. And to be honest, there are more similarities than there are differences.

I remember that learning to read was a huge thing. I recall my parents on several occasions telling me to 'be quiet' – or words to that effect – when we were travelling in the car as I made a point of reading absolutely every sign on every shop that I saw. I've found myself doing the same with Poppy.

And uniforms! I remember the excitement of getting my first school uniform in late summer before my first day in P1. This was also the last time that school uniform shopping was exciting. Every other summer after that, shopping for any school-related merchandise signalled the end of the summer holidays and was therefore accompanied by a deep dread that I felt in the pit of my stomach, usually after the first 'Back to School' sale sign went up.

Uniforms at primary school were always slightly too big. This was standard practice. Partly because at that age, growth spurts were no friend to mums, but mainly because there was not as much money knocking about. Nobody had credit as we know it now and therefore, when a purchase was made, you needed to get the absolute maximum usage out of it.

Shoes were always Clarks, and always the complete opposite of fashionable, but in primary school that didn't matter. Fashion was not on the agenda (and rightly so) when you were five years of age. It pains me to see kids of that age now and

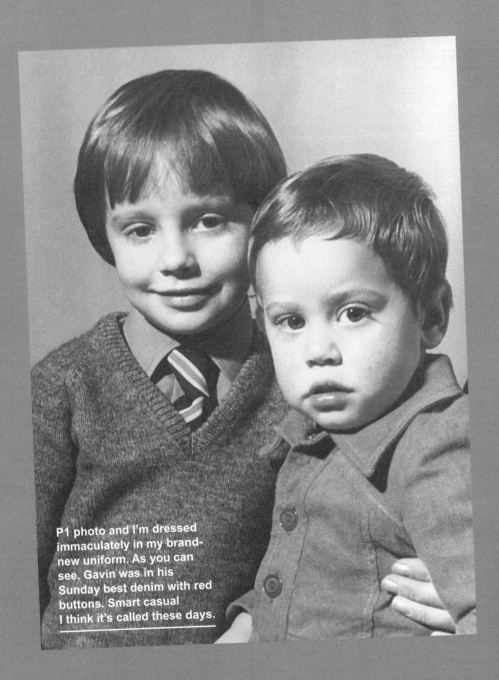

P1 photo and I'm dressed immaculately in my brand-new uniform. As you can see, Gavin was in his Sunday best denim with red buttons. Smart casual I think it's called these days.

some of them are so fashion or brand conscious. For me, kids should be allowed to be kids. They've got their whole lives to feel the pressures of peers and all the joys and pitfalls that can lead to.

# THE CANE

But anyway. Primary school was all about fun. Well, fun and discipline. I'm not sure when it changed, but there must have been a point somewhere that the respect for teachers waned slightly. Back in our day, we respected our teachers.

This was in part due to our upbringing, in part due to the times we grew up in, and in part due to the cane. Yes. An actual cane!

Now I'm not sure that it is a bad thing that there is no cane now. I'm fairly sure I would be less than thrilled if Poppy came home one day to tell me she'd been caned! But back then, it was standard practice. The mere threat of the cane was enough to keep a whole school well disciplined and playing in harmony. I actually don't ever remember anyone ever being caned in our primary school, but I do remember seeing the offending item in Mr McIlhenny's office the one time I was called there.

One day when we were in P2 there was an assembly. Mr McIlhenny breezed on to the stage in the assembly hall. He looked like a headmaster from an old movie – tall, with a black robe whooshing behind him, all formality and aura. 'We have a very serious situation, children.'

Absolute, and I mean ABSOLUTE silence in the assembly hall. You could've heard a mouse squeak, except the mice were also silent in fear.

'It has been brought to the school's attention that a GANG of boys have been seen throwing stones and getting up to mischief in the school grounds after classes have finished.'

In those days, there were usually gates and a fence or wall at a school, but these were more for aesthetic purposes, as access was sort of allowed. Many schools' playing fields were our playgrounds and football pitches in the evenings and weekends.

'This is NOT the sort of behavior we condone and WE WILL NOT PUT UP WITH IT.'

This last bit was shouted and we all sat rigidly still. Apart from wee Jamie in P1 who began to weep. I felt his pain; I wanted to weep too. I definitely needed the toilet.

WHACK! The cane came down hard on the pulpit.

We all jumped out of our oversized jumpers. More silence, broken only by more sobbing.

'Now. I am willing to give those involved a chance to redeem not just themselves, but the school and the community too. If you are a member of the Ransevyn Gang, or you know someone who is, please stand up now and you will be escorted to my office. Otherwise you will all be sent home with a note to your parents and you will all be kept behind every day for a month.'

This is where it began to unravel for me. The thing was, I was the six-year-old leader of the Ransevyn Gang. The gang was named after our housing estate in Whitehead.

It consisted of me (the boss), Gary Gardiner (age 5; lightning in his pram-wheeled go-kart, so naturally the getaway driver), Alan Gilpin (age 4 and our gadget man … his dad worked at Nortel and owned a calculator) and my little brother Gavin (age 3 and still fairly useless apart from looking cute; therefore our go-to man to get us out of trouble with adults).

I couldn't remember a specific stone-throwing incident but I do know we had attempted to make a peg gun, with varying degrees of success, and in my little P2 head, that was probably even worse than throwing stones. We often 'broke in' to the school grounds to play football. We had hit a window with our leather Mitre but it hadn't broken. Someone had seen us. Damn Gary and his two-seater pram-wheeled go-kart! I knew the rest of us would be spotted because of him. In my head we were a notorious gang of loveable yet deadly-dangerous rogues. Of course it was only a matter of time until we got caught.

So, in a room of three hundred children, one little boy dusted down his 6–7-years long grey shorts and stood up. Hand in the air, I admitted in a choked voice, 'It was me. I am the leader of the Ransevyn Gang. Let the others go.'

Gasps from all around me.

I think I enjoyed that brief moment of notoriety and respect. I could see Sarah Brisbane, my true love from P1, look at me slightly differently. It looked like admiration. Or was that adoration? I wasn't sure but I didn't care. I liked this.

The feeling lasted in and around the fifteen-second mark.

Gasps turned to sniggers. Sniggers to laughter. Laughter to hearty guffaws.

While I had been wrestling with my conscience, Mr McIlhenny had announced that he knew that the culprits were in P7 and that he would be inviting them one by one to his office. I had missed this part due to being zoned out, deciding when would be the best time to make my grand confession.

I was called to his office later that day and warned that being a gang leader was not big or clever, and that it wasn't too late for me to get back on the straight and narrow. A nod was made toward the cane sitting in the corner – when I think back, I realise that it looked like a slightly longer, more evil version of Harry Potter's wand.

That was the end of my gangland life. When I got home later that day, I called a quick meeting and it was agreed that we would change our name to 'The Famous Four'. We desperately wanted to be 'The Famous Five', but the only other person we could have enrolled was Marion, Alan's big sister, and there was NO WAY we were having a girl in our gang.

Looking back, it was all so innocent, but at the time I remember thinking that it was the worst day of my life.

Our parents sent us to school with the mindset that once we got there the teachers were the bosses. 'You listen to what your teacher tells you and God forbid I get a note back!' We would never have questioned the teachers. The message was clear and we adhered to it.

# GETTING THERE AND SCHOOL GEAR

We nearly all walked to school. In those days we went to the school that was nearest to where we lived. There was one bus, I think, that brought people to and from our school, and very few cars. Most homes had no car, and any dads that did have a car used it to go to work.

By the time P4 arrived, the beginnings of a mullet were visible, and we were allowed to freestyle on the cardigans. I went with Aunt Eileen's classic 'home-made knitted woollen sheep' number.

We nearly all had brown leather satchels. These were essentially massive, hard, leather boxes with buckles that were often the same width as the height of the person carrying them. Inside we had books. And pencil cases – proper wooden pencil cases with pens and pencils and rubbers and a compass. We didn't use the compass for anything other than inscribing our names on trees until we reached high school, but we all had one.

There were very few, if any, 'official merchandise' schoolbags back then. Your only chance to freestyle, to show your allegiance to a certain cartoon or movie, was the choice of the backing you used on your schoolbooks. That and your lunchbox.

These days it's completely different (and can be very expensive!). Last year, every girl in Poppy's class looked like she was an official walking billboard for the movie *Frozen*.

*Frozen* bags, *Frozen* coats, *Frozen* lunchboxes, pens, pencils, rubbers, book coverings, crayons – you name it, it was plastered in *Frozen*. A problem arose with the arrival of *Moana* and *Trolls*. Suddenly *Frozen* was so last year, and all the parents had a load of merchandise they needed to get rid of and replace with the latest trend. We didn't suffer from this problem in our day.

I do remember being slightly mortified at my book covering, though. The 'rich kids' had *Superman* lunchboxes and book backing. It was one of the first movies (along with maybe *Star Wars*) that had a few merchandising bits and pieces. I could only dream of such items. I had *Captain Pugwash* wallpaper in my bedroom. I loved that programme and was delighted with my wallpaper. I loved my books being backed in the few bits that were spare, too, right up until I saw R2-D2 covering Peter Gilmour's books and I instantly wanted that.

I was not alone in having books that mirrored my parents' taste in home decorating. Woodchip wallpaper was massive back then and I often had this as my covering. I always ended up picking it off, though, and my books looked a mess. Worse still, I'd forget to close my satchel properly on a rainy day. Woodchip wallpaper is very absorbent and I learned the hard way: always remember to close your school bag.

There is a high percentage of adults in Northern Ireland of a certain age who suffer from chronic back pain. I'm convinced this is the generation of woodchippers who forgot to close their satchels.

Primary school also featured a type of 'bag' that I have never really seen a version of since; so much so that I am not entirely sure that I haven't made it up. It was a kind of luminous, plastic–rubber hybrid with a tie string. It was used solely for either sports gear (shorts, white T-shirt and black gutties), or for your recorder. The PE version was slightly bigger, obviously; the recorder one, well, it was the shape of the recorder. Without an explanation, I'm not sad to see these go.

Captain Pugwash! The best wallpaper and book coverings I ever had … right up until they became the worst wallpaper and book coverings ANYONE ever had.

# TECHNOLOGY

There was technology back then. Not as we know it now, but it was technology nonetheless.

I remember the first time any of us ever saw a calculator. The reaction would have been no different if Buck Rogers' sidekick Twiki had come waddling in to our classroom. We all gathered round to see this futuristic marvel. It had quite large buttons, as I remember, and the numbers were red LED.

'This piece of equipment can process any mathematical problem you give it –' Mr Gordon paused with a degree of dramatic flair before announcing – 'instantly.'

'Oooooh.' We were suitably impressed and gasped as one.

'Watch –' another dramatic pause – 'this.'

$$123x56+346/23x23.5 = 7{,}391.26$$

Holy shit! That really was impressive. Our reaction, however, was somewhat muted as we had no fucking clue what the answer should be.

Mr Gordon, sensing he was losing his recently acquired status of technological wizard, quickly typed in 11x11 = 121 (we were doing our 11 times tables at the time) and we all stood up in disbelief, clapping and puffing our cheeks out at one another.

'Quare job, that,' said Alan Paisley as he blew his cheeks out, shaking his head in disbelief. Alan's dad was a farmer and he always had grown-up man reactions to things that I found intriguing. 'They'll take over the world, ya know.' He may have been psychic too.

The first time you saw a photo taken by cameras like this was when the girl in Boots handed them to you. No 'oh-God-no-delete-THAT' in those days.

I always think it's funny that in order for technology to impress us we have to get it to do something we already know. Years later Michael McIntyre (one of my favourite comedians) did a brilliant sketch about how amazing Google Earth is and how it's almost beyond belief that by simply dragging a mouse and clicking a button we can be instantly whisked to any place on the planet. And the first place we try out is our own house – which we could of course simply walk out of, and turn and look at. Essentially my class did this with the calculator in 1983.

# PE

PE was one of our favourite things to do in school. I don't think that has changed for most kids since our day. But when I was wee, we did the most random things during PE.

There was a wooden climbing-frame type thing that attached to the wall of the assembly hall, and that swung out and fixed to the floor when it was PE day. This thing went floor to ceiling and from memory, yeah, it was attached to the floor but it just swayed at the top. Health and safety would have a meltdown these days but, it was back then, and this kind of kit was standard. I vaguely remember there being a safety mat of sorts, although not the kind you see these days. Think a thin, pale blue, rubberised rug. Basically, if you came down too fast, you felt it. There were also ropes hanging from the ceiling. These were tied back during normal classes, but released on PE days. 'Get up there

tahellathat' was the cry from the teacher. There was a piece of coloured tape at the top of the rope that we had to touch before either dropping on to the rubber rug, resulting in a bruise at best, a sprain or break at worst, or the slide technique, which always resulted in third degree burns.

One day wee Willy Bunter came a cropper. (Sadly for Willy, his name rhymed with Billy, and he was carrying a few extra pounds. He wasn't massively overweight, but in the 80s, sometimes that's all it took.) Struggling even to get his second foot off the rug on to the rope, he was sent up the wooden climbing frame. As he struggled to the top, it started to sway, and the more he panicked, the more it swayed, until it made a cracking sound, and unhooked from its floor anchor. I'll never forget the fear in his eyes as it began to swing slowly back towards the breeze-block wall.

'Scale down. Scale down, Willy!'

We could hear the panic in the teacher's voice but wee Willy Bunter's sausage fingers were locked on to that top bar like a limpet. He was not going to be scaling down any time soon. The climbing frame began to gather speed and we could all see what was going to happen. Well, when I say we could see what was going to happen, it was through eyes swimming with tears as we were all pissing ourselves laughing. You know that half-scared, half-funny laugh? That one.

'Wee Willy is going to hit that wall some skelp,' said Alan, in his weird, grown-up, farmer-chat style. This made us all laugh even more. Everyone was now laughing apart from the teacher and wee Willy.

WHACK.

He hit the wall and bounced out slightly. Bounced again. A less intense bump this time.

Then it stopped. Wee Willy was trapped like a Bunter sandwich between the wall and the frame. Just his wee crying face peeking out from between the rails.

It was terrible. Awful. My God it was funny.

'Okay, William?' said the teacher, more in hope than expectation.

Prince Charming, Adam Ant
If You Let Me Stay, Terence Trent D'Arby
With a Little Help From My Friends, Wet Wet Wet
Manic Monday, The Bangles
Superman theme
Video Killed the Radio Star, The Buggles
The Only Way is Up, Yazz
I Think We're Alone Now, Tiffany
Glory of Love, Peter Cetera
(Everything I Do) I Do It For You, Bryan Adams

SCHOOL MIX TAPE

'Aahhhh ... Not really, teacher.'

'You'll be fine. Just listen to me. Begin to climb down slowly. I'll be at the bottom to catch you.'

We looked at each other. Nobody fancied the teacher's chances if Willy jumped. And then we heard a gasp and a whimper as wee Willy Bunter launched down like an out-of-control roller coaster. His back skidding against the wall, his wee chin catching **EVERY** rail on the way down, and the sound ... oh, it is the sound that I'll never forget. If you have ever gone down steps on a bicycle as a kid and made a noise whilst doing so, it was a bit like that, only slower and with pain involved.

'Aaaaaaaahabadahabadahabada ...'

**THUMP**.

There was blood everywhere.

The screams of both Willy and the teacher were only drowned out by the nervous laughter of the rest of us who felt we'd just witnessed something we would never see again. Willy said that he caught his chin on the teacher's bottom row of teeth, who, he claimed, had his mouth wide open, screaming as Willy landed.

None of the rest of us could be sure. He needed stitches in his chin, and went from being something of a nerd to something of a hero. We all got a note to take home the following day and the frame never did make an appearance again whilst I was at primary school. I saw him recently and he still has the battle scar, although I suspect he doesn't tell people where or how he acquired it. (He's very successful and quite well known in his field!)

Primary school is something of a rose-tinted blur after that. Playgrounds consisted of footballs and jumpers as goalposts. British bulldogs and kiss chase for the older ones. There were no iPads or gadgets back then. (Actually, a friend of ours had an eye pad, but it was a massive plaster worn under huge NHS glasses and it was to correct a spectacular squint. His nickname was Cock-eyed Colin ... which was cruel and not even relevant as his first name was Andrew.)

Kick the Can, First Light and Kerby were all games we spent hours playing and the only thing that needed recharged in order to play was yourself and your mates. Recharging usually involved a jam sandwich and tap water (mixy-upy orange if you were lucky) and back outside before your mum had time to shout, 'Be back before it gets dark.'

# THE SUMMER BEFORE SECONDARY SCHOOL

Secondary school was different. Suddenly we became aware. Aware of what we wore, aware of how we spoke, aware of how we looked in general, aware of what music we listened to, what labels we had access to. We became ... teenagers.

We also became aware of GIRLS.

I remember watching one of my favourite comedians, Eddie Izzard, who summed things up pretty much perfectly: At the very moment you want to look your best, sound your best and smell your best, God strikes you down with ... puberty – and at the precise moment you want all of these things, you will never look worse, sound worse or smell worse.

That came later though. The first thing that we had to negotiate in school was not being 'flushed'.

'Yeah,' said a spotty, slightly hairy-faced Andy from up the street, chewing chewing gum and smoking one of his dad's Regals whilst trying hard not to cough and cry through the

Standard practice on your last day at school – write all over each other's shirts. This only happened once, on the very last day. If you even came home with an ink stain on your shirt before then, you were in BIG trouble.

obviously terrible combination. 'We can't wait 'til the first years arrive coz we just take them all into the bogs and flush their heads down the toilets. They always cry but we don't care.'

He began a coughing fit and we thought he was going to be sick. He was obviously enjoying the attention he was getting from the crowd of P7s who were about to go to his school slightly more than the cigarette which we thought might kill him then and there.

'Got this flippin' cold and it's given me a terrible flu ... coughing all the time. It's not the smoking. I love smoking,' he said through bloodshot eyes, with tears streaming down his cheeks.

Andy would later go on to become a minister of the church, and a rather nice guy altogether. I doubt he still smokes, or flushes people's heads down the toilet for that matter.

Anyway, these stories meant only one thing that summer. We had to learn to fight boys much bigger than ourselves. This meant watching *Rocky* and *The Karate Kid*. Having hired both out on two separate occasions, we thought we had learned enough and were confident that some 'left-a-circle, wax-on-wax-off' would see us through the hard times. Of course there never was any 'flushing' but the thought of it ruined our summer holiday before big school. Well, until we watched those movies and realised that nobody in there would be a match for us.

**TOP 10 MOVIES**
1 **The Karate Kid**
2 **Raiders of the Lost Ark**
3 **Batman (Michael Keaton and Jack Nicholson)**
4 **Beverly Hills Cop**
5 **Nightmare on Elm Street**
6 **Superman**
7 **Star Wars, Empire Strikes Back and Return of the Jedi**
8 **Terminator**
9 **Back to the Future**
10 **The Lost Boys**

# REBELLION

As you get older and start to find yourself, there tends to be a type of rebelliousness that creeps into your personality. Some students would go too far but I always had a bit too much respect for the teachers. And by respect for the teachers, I of course mean fear of my parents because woe betide me if I got a note home or, worse, if they were asked to come in to the school. I kept a fairly clean slate.

Most of us did. Compared to what I hear about going on in schools these days, there was little in the way of rebellion. 'Mitching off' was about the worst thing that I ever did and, of course, it ended in disaster. My two best friends in school, Alan and Jason, and I had planned to take one of the days late in the summer term off. Alan had sneaked a half-bottle of whisky from his dad's revolving globe, drink-cabinet thing. Jason had been syphoning Pernod from the bar that his parents had in their garage. He had been swapping it for water. Slowly. Systematically. Brilliantly.

We were working class, and any alcohol that was in our house was bought for consumption on the night, so I brought the mixer. Which was milk. Look, it was all I could find, and to be honest, we didn't really care. The plan was set. I got dressed in my school clothes as normal before leaving at the usual time.

'Bye, Mum. Just heading to school here.'

'Yes, Stephen, I know that.'

'Okay, might go to Alan's after school. You know after we go to school, we might go to Alan's after school.'

'Okay, Stephen. Just be back for tea.'

'Will do.'

The conversation was mirrored at Alan's and Jason's houses. We met at the barley field on a hot summer's morning and proceeded to get pretty drunk on whisky, Pernod and milk. We had bought eight bags of Meanies and so had everything we could've possibly needed to sustain us through the day.

What a great day that was! Drunkenly laughing at everything, discussing girls and generally thinking we would own the world when we grew up. Where our genius plan had fallen flat, though, was that although we had told our parents we were going to school, we had forgotten that the teachers would notice that we weren't actually there. We knew we were smarter than the teachers,

but we hadn't taken into consideration that the three of us all off together might arouse suspicion.

It did.

And when we all finally got home (thankfully pretty sober since our drink had run out by 11 a.m.) we had some fairly irate parents waiting for us.

All three of us were punished severely by our mums and dads.

All three of us sat down very gingerly on our hard plastic seats the next day.

All three of us were put in detention.

All three of us never did it again.

# DATING

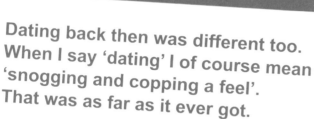

Dating back then was different too. When I say 'dating' I of course mean 'snogging and copping a feel'. That was as far as it ever got.

Actually for me, there was little in the way of feeling anything bar sore gums due to my enamel-cracking, teeth-knocking snogging style. 'French kissing' was the thing at school when we were teenagers. What the fuck was French kissing?!? How the hell would I know?!? There was no Google back then so we relied on second-hand information from mates and listening in on older kids' conversations.

'Yeah, I slipped the tongue' was a common expression. **SLIPPED THE TONGUE WHERE?** I remember thinking in horror. Steenson was a hit with the ladies, so I asked him, but was obviously just 'asking for a friend'.

'Yeah, Clem, just stick your tongue in her mouth. She'll love it.'

Okay. Sounded easy. Didn't see the French connection, but was happier with this explanation than with that given by one of the older kids who was telling us it involved garlic bulbs and a beret. That obviously was someone taking the piss, but I literally was SO clueless that I considered it. Louise from Fifth Year will never know just how close she was to being met by a garlic-infused younger me, in a black and white striped T-shirt, wearing my mum's beret. But my mum spotted the young Inspector Clouseau leaving the house one evening and went through me for a shortcut for taking her beret and her T-shirt.

**'GET BACK IN THIS HOUSE NOW!'**

'Shell' Suit
3  £44.99

'Shell' Top
1  £38.99

'Shell' Pants £22.99
2

'Shell Suits' - the latest in leisure fashion; lightweight two-tier fabrics fashioned for versatility, strength and comfort.

1

Puma Green/Dark Grey 'shell-style' Top with concealable hood. Made from lightweight woven fabric with a soft Nylon lining. Two colour drawcords at collar and waist with 'Puma' toggles. Large centre pocket with Velcro flap. Two side pockets. Embroidered logo. Shell: POLYESTER 65%, COTTON 35%, Lined NYLON.

21G 26W Green 'Shell' Top

Order chest sizes:
36/38 39/41 42/44 46 ins.

£38.99

2

Puma Dark Grey/Green 'shell-style' Trousers made from lightweight woven fabric with soft Cotton lining. Elasticated waist with two colour drawcord. Puma woven badge on waistband and two side pockets. Elasticated at ankles. Shell: POLYESTER 65%, COTTON 35%. Lined COTTON.

'Shell' Suit
4  £56.99

21D 28W Green 'Shell' Pants

Order sizes: 30 32 34 36/38 ins.

£22.99

568

With hindsight, I suspect she knew what I was planning and was stopping me from making a merde of myself.

In those days, you hoped for some sort of snogging at a Blue Lamp Disco, or at the youth club. There was little by way of preparation. You put on your best shellsuit, splashed on your dad's Brut 33, and hoped for the best.

Always hoped. Never expected.

As I got older, there were a few exceptions. A couple of times I'd arranged dates.

We arranged to 'meet'. The meeting place was invariably at the front of the library near where we lived. Remember too that once the 'date' had been arranged, there were no mobile phones so no texting 'I'm running late', or 'Sorry, I can't make it'.

No, you made the arrangement and you stuck to it.

Or you didn't.

How many couples would be with the person they are with now if their date had turned up? Or if they'd waited that wee bit longer? Or had been able to let the other person know, 'My cat has died and I just can't face your tongue rammed in my mouth'?

We'll never know.

What I personally remember is that it was a lot more innocent back then. Even as we got older, we had to learn the skill of chatting a woman up. Okay, this usually meant Dutch courage and asking if they fancied a dance during the notorious 'erection section' ...

As the club (okay, discotheque) was in full flow, the DJ would **STOP EVERYTHING** and announce in a suitably cringeworthy American accent that it was time to slow things down. Everyone sloped off to the sides of the dancefloor, as the opening chords of the Bryan Adams classic 'Everything I Do' filled the smoky room. It was time for action!

Looking back, I'm fairly sure that this is what musical chairs was designed to train you for. It was the same feeling of excited panic. As soon as the music slowed, and the lights went down, we ran about like blue-arsed flies trying to find someone – ANYONE – to dance with.

There was no Tinder to swipe. No guarantees. You usually had a mental list of the top five girls you'd seen busting moves to 'Rhythm is a Dancer'.

Waistcoats, mullets, and the glitterballs were not for retro effect – they were there to try and create some sort of Americanised disco atmosphere from the very basic lighting systems that were in place.

You gambled. You gambled that you were on **THEIR** list, and also, that as you were rejected (in descending numerical order) that the later numbers hadn't seen you being rejected and realised they weren't first choice, undermining your already slim chance of success, even with the mid-table numbers.

It wasn't easy and I was crap at chatting up anyway. The fact that my voice didn't break until I was seventeen didn't help matters (although one bonus was that my high-pitched squeak was easily audible in the noisy disco).

'Hiya! I was wonder ... '

'No.'

'Right. Okay. No problem sure.'

Go for number 2.

'Hiya! I wa ... '

'Fuck off.'

'Yeah. Sure thing. No problem'

Number 3

[Tap her on the shoulder.]

'Hiy ...' I trailed off as I saw Lawrence French kissing her.

Number 4 then.

'Before you even come near me, ya wee ballbag, I've already seen you asking about four girls to dance so fuck off if you think I'm anybody's sloppy seconds.'

'No problem.'

Balls.

No matter how the night went (and invariably it ended with me standing awkwardly by while Steenson or Lawrence or any of my good-looking mates French kissed my numbers 1, 2, 3 AND 4), there was always Spuds. Yes, it was primarily a food outlet in Belfast, but it also doubled as the Last Chance Saloon. Many a snog I had in there with girls who didn't make the top 10 (and who I am quite certain wouldn't have had me on **THEIR** list). But there was a mutual, unwritten understanding that, as we stood swaying, waiting on the bus home, we should unite in failure by grabbing a kiss, before, **ALWAYS** before, getting wired into our cheesy-beany baked potato. We knew things hadn't worked out in the disco, but we weren't prepared to French kiss post-spud.

Looking back, it was all fairly innocent and boring compared to the Tinder dating scene I hear stories about. I'm sure young people these days have far more success on the dating scene, but do they get a baked potato after? I doubt it.

# Chapter Seven

# FASHION AND HOME

# TERRY TOWELLING AND SUN-IN

So while secondary school was partly about pushing boundaries, it was also definitely about becoming aware of yourself – and painfully aware of what other people thought of you. Fashion was suddenly a word I knew about.

For school we had a uniform but we had options. Yeah, black trousers – but it didn't stipulate the style! Cue '20 pleats'. These beauties did exactly what they said on the tin: they were tight at the ankles but with twenty pleats at the top. When we stood they looked to all intents and purposes like a regular trouser, but a flick of the hand in your pocket, or a gust of wind and whoosh – you were MC-fucking-Hammer, baby!

Winkle-picker shoes and white terry-towelling socks were compulsory with these trousers. Our ties had to be done back to front with the skinny bit hanging down, and our grey jumpers were, by preference, Slazenger. The white sock phenomenon didn't last too long – there was soon a note sent home barring them.

The accompanying hairstyle was one of a few available. Streaks were banned but you could just about get

When in Italy, style capital of Europe, it's important to set off your Man Utd shorts and socks with a plain white T-shirt. I think the addition of the stripy woollen waistcoat completed the look perfectly.

The important thing when getting home-made 'tips' in your hair was never to be photographed. As you can see, I failed miserably. Note the half-analogue/half-digital watch and Chicago Bears American football shirt. I was still single at this stage, incidentally.

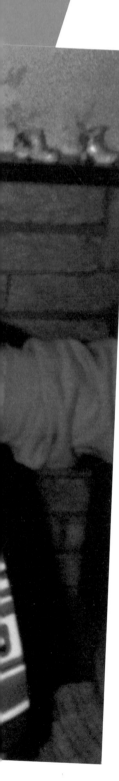

away with a blonde tuft at the front. Alan went with a loose perm at one stage, based on INXS's lead singer Michael Hutchence's look. He was good enough looking to get away with it. I tried on one occasion, but as my hair was shorter, I ended up looking more like I was wearing a helmet. Jason Donovan was huge in these days and my friend Jason aspired to be like him. We all did. Jason had naturally fair hair and so with a little bit of Sun-In, he quickly BECAME Jason Donovan. Aha! This was my chance. Okay, I couldn't carry off a perm, but Sun-In was a gift, plus my mum already had some. I just added a WEEEEEEEE bit of extra lemon juice and waited.

I looked more like Mick Hucknall and I certainly didn't suit being a ginger.

So eventually I landed on what I thought was my perfect style. I kept a fairly sensible semi-mullet look on the top and sides, but let a finger's width of hair grow at the back – the GENIUS behind the style; the rat's tail. I had this style until I was sixteen. I never had a girlfriend until I was sixteen. Coincidence. I am sure it was merely coincidence.

All of these hairstyles were done by Mum at home, and often involved the use of a cereal bowl as a guide. Back in our day, hair dyeing involved a kind of skull cap with holes in it. Mum would jab a pen-shaped hook device into the hole to pull several strands of hair through the cap at a time. This was a painful experience, and once you had absolutely reached your pain threshold, she would bring out the bleach.

Not bleach as we know it, but a kind of pastel purple gunk with a similar consistency to custard, but with the smell of a highly toxic turd. It was an unpleasant experience and, although I was 100 per cent certain that I would look like Pat Sharp from *Fun House* at the end and suddenly become irresistible to the female population, the process was challenging. Certainly you would not want your photo taken during it …

Cameras were brought out if ANY new clothing was bought for us. Here we have a new patterned jumper and brown bell-bottom combo. Stylish, yet practical.

It's clear I'm raging here as a) Gavin has cool patterned pyjamas and I have a red silk number, and b) the trousers are WAY too short and Christmas was miles away.

# LEVI'S

The absolute pinnacle of fashion, and something I could never afford, were Levi's 501s. Adverts on TV were always just adverts, but then Levi's changed the game with their sexy music-driven campaigns, featuring handsome cool men.

**501**

**THE ORIGINAL SHRINK-TO-FIT JEANS.**

We all wanted to look like the guy from the Levi's adverts. Sadly, I never did and now more resemble the guy sitting next to him. I tried the underwear and socks combo, but it didn't work well for me, standing in my Y-fronts in the outhouse with our dog Zico trying to mount my calf. Luckily, that moment wasn't captured.

EVERYONE had to have a pair. The red tab of the 501s was more than a fashion statement – it was announcing to the world, and to girls in particular: 'THE WEARER OF THESE IS A STUD.'

'I bet you're wonderin' how I knew ... DAN DAN DAN DUHHHHHH ... I heard it through the grapevine.'

I NEEDED A PAIR OF THESE. The absence of them in my wardrobe was obviously the reason why I didn't have a girlfriend.

'Mum. Dad. I've something I need to tell you.'

'I told you, Helen. We shouldn't have let him grow that bloody ponytail! For fuck's sake. No grandchildren!'

'What are you talking about?'

I had no idea what he was on about and looked at him with complete disgust the way teenagers do. He knew NOTHING!

'Mum. Dad. I NEED a new pair of jeans.'

'Aye, well, right enough, Roy, his jeans are a bit small for him.'

'Fine. I'll pick you up a new pair on my way home from work. What time does Dunnes close, love?'

Dunnes? DUNNES?!? What the fuck is wrong with him? Does he want me to be the laughing stock of the next Blue Lamp Disco?

'No. I need a pair of Levi's 501s. You know like in the advert where the fella takes his off and washes them and sits in his underwear while they dry? Those ones. Please.'

'That fella is wearing SHORTS underneath his jeans. He's not even wearing pants, son. It's some sort of auld American nonsense. Don't be watching that.'

Boxer shorts were only just bursting on to the scene. We all wore Y-fronts. My parents didn't approve of American stuff. This was going to prove more difficult than I had imagined.

'But everyone in school is wearing them.'

'If everyone in school put their head in a fire, would you?'

I always hated that question because there was only ever one answer that you could give which was 'Of course not, no.' If you ever tried to be a smart arse and say yes, it would have ended in a swift and painful punshiment for a) talking back and b) being a smart arse.

'Well, no, I wouldn't, but I would really love a pair of Levi's like EVERYONE in school has. Please.'

'Pass me that Kays catalogue there, Helen.'

Before the internet and Google, the only way of pricing something was to look it up in the catalogue.

**'FIFTY-FIVE FUCKING POUNDS?** Unless they are made of gold, the answer is no. Are they made of gold?'

Another stupid bloody leading question.

I looked down at the floor and hated them with every sinew of my being.

'Sure if I win the pools this weekend, I'll buy us a pair each.'

There was no Lottery to reference back then, it was either the pools or premium bonds.

'Ach well, Roy, it is his birthday soon so maybe ...'

Grunt. 'We'll see ... Go to bed.'

Fast forward a few weeks and I did get a pair of Levi's. I could not believe it! They had actually gone to a shop and bought me a pair of **ACTUAL LEVI'S** 50' – oh my God, what the fuck are these – '8s.' They had an **ORANGE TAB? FUUUUUUUUUUCKKKKKKKK!**

Looking back, this was the least grateful moment of my life. We were genuinely working class, and buying these jeans would have been a big deal to my parents, and they would have been so thrilled that they had got them for me.

And I, like a spoilt wee brat, couldn't even bring myself to be grateful. Thinking about it now, I want to slap my teenage self hard on the rear, with the crap belt they bought me to hold them up.

As my parents handed me the jeans, I held them like you might hold a dead mouse. By its tail. Forefinger and thumb. Held away from my body in disgust. I tried my best to look grateful and kissed my mum and dad, and said, 'I **LOVE** them!' (I hated them) and 'I love you both so much!' (I hated them both so much) and 'I'll never wear anything else!' (I'll wear **ANYTHING** else apart from these). What an ungrateful wee shit!

However karma had the last laugh on this occasion. In a desperate attempt to make my new jeans into 501s, a mate of mine ripped a back pocket off a pair in American Madness in town and gave me the red tab from them (I paid him £3). He used to do the odd bit of bad stuff 'to order'.

Anyway, I set about cutting the orange tab from mine with the plan being that I'd stitch the red tab on, and Bob would be my fashionable uncle. In the midst of cutting off the offending orange tab, though, I put the scissors through both the denim and the sofa I was leaning on, resulting in a sore rear for slicing the sofa, and a spectacular 'if-you-don't-like-these-fucking-jeans-they-are-going-in-this-fucking-bin' ceremony. I cried, even at the ripe old age of sixteen, and never again have I ever been ungrateful (for even the shittest present).

My cousin Simon and I are a similar age and often dressed similarly. Here he is wearing the fashionable 'Rupert the Bear' jean. It would be another eighteen months before I sported a pair of these beauties.

# THE PHONE

At around this time the phone was beginning to make itself a part of our lives more and more. Even the most old-school families were getting one.

Remembering phone numbers was a skill that those who grew up in the 70s and 80s will be familiar with. To be fair, we had to remember them as there was nowhere to store them unless you had a wee black book. Of course Mum and Dad had a wee tattered book with the letters of the alphabet cut into the right-hand side of the pages for quick and easy access, but there was no way that we would be putting Shirley's or Lesley-Anne's number into **THAT**!

To this day I can still remember the home numbers of about ten of my friends' parents' although I'm fairly sure they wouldn't work now. For a start, numbers were a lot shorter then. No prefixes to speak of really. Calling

mates or potential girlfriends when you got a little older was an expensive hobby. Ringing your mates was always a call that lasted in and around the 20- to 45-second mark, and the length of time was dictated mainly by who answered. If it was your mate's mum, you had the ten-second polite 'Hello, Mrs Steenson, is Alan at home?'

[Wait for 15 seconds.]

'All right, Clem, what's happening?'

'You coming out tonight? Football at the cricky field in 20 minutes.'

'Aye.'

[And hang up.]

With potential girlfriends, calls could last a lot longer, although a lot of that time was listening to her chat about her mates being 'a bit slutty

and going to second base' and me just mainly grunting and sitting in silence.

The nightmare was when the phone bill came in. Not in the early days, of course, when the bill was the bill. £45 for the quarter or whatever it was. It was when those bastards at British Telecom brought in itemised billing that the proverbial shit hit the fan. Up until then, my mum usually got, 'Helen, the phone bill was quite high this month,' to which she'd reply, 'That's strange ... I thought I'd only used it a couple of times,' as I sniggered away about the fact that I'd got away with the crime of the century – ringing Louise for almost an hour!

That practice ended fairly sharpish with the introduction of the itemised bill. I remember so clearly how I found out that those British Telecom eggheads had introduced it.

Bill comes in.

Take no notice and go out and play football in the front garden.

Dad arrives home.

I hear from inside the house: '**WHAT THE FUCK** is this? Sixty-three pounds for a phone bill? Fuck Buzby and his bloody adverts.'

I shake my head dismissively and continue playing with Gavin. 'Flipping Mum must be using the phone all the time, bro!'

'Yeah ... sounds like a lot of money.'

Then I hear '**NINE-TWO-SEVEN-FUCKING-EIGHT!**'

Continue playing football with Gavin but somewhere in the back of my mind I'm thinking, those numbers sound familiar.

It hits me, just about the same time as the front door bursts open to reveal my dad, red-faced and holding a fistful of papers. I haven't seen him look this angry since Gavin (and by Gavin, I mean ME) left the immersion heater on in the summer of 1984.

Each piece of paper has 📞 at the top and a picture of that annoying wee Buzby bird. There really did seem to be quite a lot of them. I die a little inside as I am swept indoors by my dad who has me by the collar. I'm thrown on to the sofa whilst I'm read out a series of dates and times and amounts ...

I went to bed with a sore behind that night. I wanted to call Louise and tell her the bad news, but decided it wasn't a good time.

Make someone happy.

# POLICE 6

I'll never forget Keith Burnside on the real-life crime stoppers TV show *Police 6*, and have laughed playing the audio clip back on Q Radio. This was a brilliantly crap TV show which I assume came about because of the Troubles.

As the news back then was dominated by bombs and shootings and arrests and atrocities, there was never any time for normal crime ... cue *Police 6*! Every Sunday Keith would sit in a brown suit, on a brown set, and look very serious whilst reading out the 'crimes' that had happened that week, encouraging us to come forward with information.

Now, I don't know if it was because the criminal masterminds in NI had been assimilated into the 'organisations' or that the said 'organisations' semi-policed their own areas, but the crimes were never

terribly, well, bad. I remember it often being said back in the day that, ironically enough, Northern Ireland was one of the safest places for tourists to visit as there was no 'real crime'. However, the Troubles being beamed across the world was not the best advert for the place and so we never really got to find out.

In fact, during one of the worst periods of the Troubles, I remember a Mediterranean family being spotted outside Carrickfergus Castle. No word of a lie (and this was before the days of social media so it was literally through the grapevine) – locals started to go to the castle to catch a glimpse of these foreigners. The tourists had become the attraction. And **EVERYONE** loved them. I'm fairly sure that they ended up back on the train with more weight in gifted soda breads, Guinness and Coleraine cheddar than any flight would allow you to carry on.

Anyway, back to Keith: 'A set of cufflinks have been stolen from a golf club in Omagh some time between Monday 3rd and Tuesday 18th of May. The secretary said he left them on the window ledge next to the typewriter. If you know the whereabouts of these cufflinks, please call Omagh police on, Omagh 8796.'

**AND THAT WAS IT!** The whole number right there!

It got even better when someone found something. 'A bag of bowling balls has been found near the VG shop on the Hightown Road. The bag features a brass plate with the inscription "To Dessie Maynard, the best damn bowler that Aughnocloy has ever seen".' There then follows a video clip of the bowls, the inscription and every other detail that a bag of

U Can't Touch This, MC Hammer
Need You Tonight, INXS
Too Many Broken Hearts, Jason Donovan
Money's Too Tight (To Mention), Simply Red
I Heard It Through the Grapevine, Marvin Gaye
Relax, Frankie Goes to Hollywood
Karma Chameleon, Culture Club
Call Me, Spagna
Wake Me Up Before You Go-Go, Wham!
Teenage Kicks, The Undertones

**HOME MIX TAPE**

Our TV with no remote. If you needed to change the channel, you had to get up. Also, the aerial had to be relocated depending on which of the four channels you were watching. Think that's *Eastenders* on at Christmas?

bowling balls could possibly have, at which point Keith says, 'So if you know Dessie, or you are in fact Dessie, please call North Queen Street police on Belfast 4512 with an accurate description of the aforementioned bowls and bag, and they are there for you to collect.' He had just given us every single detail!

# BACK IN OUR DAY

*Police* 6 was utter genius. We loved it in our house and I think partly it was down to the fact that it reminded us that we lived in an okay place. Like a really okay place!

Yes, all 'that' stuff was going on but we grew up during it so we had no frame of reference for anything better or worse. It was just living to us. *Police 6,* the crap TV show with no budget and no crimes, comforted us all – probably on some sub-conscious level – that we lived in a really lovely place. In a lovely time. It seems so strange to describe it as such but it was essentially a lot simpler back then.

If we wanted something we saved.

If we wanted to tell our friends something, we met them (or phoned them, but as you know that was **VERY** expensive).

We talked about what was happening on TV, in the cinema, in school, in work, wherever, face to face.

We all looked out for each other and we all laughed together far more than I remember us crying together.

Is everything remembered through rose-tinted spectacles? Maybe.

Times were tough.

Northern Ireland was not an easy place to live in at times and everyone knows someone affected by the bad stuff.

But it moulded who we are today.

The greater 'WE' that our newfound friends – 'tourists' – rave about.

Our crap hair, awful clothes, home-made food, rubbish cars, wick TV shows ... they created the people who, despite the Troubles, created an environment that enabled a peaceful time in Northern Ireland.

The Northern Ireland that, despite our size, punches above its weight in industry, politics, sport, the arts, music, television and movies.

The Northern Ireland that Liam Neeson sells to the world in our super-sexy tourist advert is the one that **YOU** and I created.

We played outside, we got excited by the school trolley with the TV on it even though we knew we were in for some god-awful programme about trees.

We were scared shitless by Vincent Price's voice in those public information films about playing near water, or climbing on to electricity pylons.

We were there for the invention of the computer but none of us knew (some of us still don't) how to use them or what to use them for.

We sniggered at 7-inch floppys and we didn't really know why.

*Tomorrow's World* featured stuff like 'barcodes replacing stick-on prices' and while our parents scoffed, all we wanted to know was why the hell we were watching *Tomorrow's World* when *The Krypton Factor* was on the other channel.

Shouting 'Fred, there's no bread' and 'Hey Lawrence, a pint of Harp and a packet of dates' instantly made you a world-class mimic.

Jim Megaw and Jimmy Cricket were superstars.

The Europa was the most bombed hotel in Europe and we told **EVERYONE** (and still do) with a kind of weird solemn pride.

We had *Dungeons and Dragons* books where we chose what happened, but always folded our pages just in case we died on page 58.

Friends were actual real people, and the only time you would see pictures of anyone's dinner was if it was inadvertently caught on camera in the obligatory Christmas shot of Nana and Aunt Eileen in their paper hats.

We don't have a digital diary of the life we have lived. We didn't have Facebook, or Snapchat, or Twitter, or Instagram or Insta-face-snap-tweet-a-gram or whatever the hell the latest 'in' social media thing is.

We simply have a few faded photos and a bunch of brilliant memories ... of the good old days.

# Acknowledgements

Thanks to Colin Murray for writing
the foreword; Robert Walshe, MD at
Q Radio, for his unwavering support;
Helen Wright from Blackstaff for
asking me to write the book, and
talking me back from the edge every
time I was about to throw the head up.

Thanks also to all of my friends who
are featured (please don't sue); my
parents and my brother Gavin, and
my (almost) brother Lawrence who I
laughed so hard with that I was glad
of the tight Y-fronts.

This book is for everyone who grew
up in Northern Ireland during these
times – who lived it, loved it, hated it,
and loved it again. Thanks for helping
to bring back such fond memories.